T0312144

THE AFFORDABLE HOUSING MARKET IN INDIA

This book examines the housing crisis in India and underlines the need for formal affordable housing markets. India is home to the world's largest population of slum dwellers. The book examines actual causes of the problem, and the financial and political issues which underlie it. The volume:

- Analyses multiple perspectives on affordable housing from the points of view of slum dwellers, builders, facilitators, bureaucrats, and politicians
- Presents a fresh overview of the housing sector in India based on the conditions of slum dwellers in a typical, medium-sized, fast-growing city – Raipur, in the state of Chhattisgarh
- Puts forward radical conclusions, practical solutions, and policy recommendations for a formal affordable housing market in India

This will be a major intervention for scholars and researchers of urban sociology, built environment, public policy, development studies, economics, political economy, institutional economics, and urban studies as well as policymakers, planners, and professionals in the urban development sector.

Padmini Ram is Assistant Professor, School of Business Studies and Social Sciences, Christ University, Bengaluru, India and Principal Investigator, Christ–LabourNet Academic Research Endeavour (CLARE), an industry–academia collaboration working on informal economy. With over 17 years of experience in various sectors of public policy and development in India and abroad, she combines the rigour of an academic researcher and the pragmatic approach of a practitioner. She holds a PhD from the University of Cambridge, and her research papers have been published in several reputed international journals.

Malcolm Harper is Emeritus Professor of Enterprise Development, School of Management, Cranfield University, UK. He was educated at Oxford, Harvard, and Nairobi. Since 1995 he has worked independently, mainly in India. He has published extensively on enterprise development, micro-finance, and livelihoods. He was Chairman of Basix Finance in India for 10 years and is Chairman of M-CRIL/EDA of New Delhi, the international microfinance and social rating company. He is chair, trustee, and board member of various institutions in the United Kingdom, the Netherlands, the United States, and India, and has worked on issues of poverty across the world.

THE AFFORDABLE HOUSING MARKET IN INDIA

Institutional Constraints, Informal
Sector and Privatisation

Padmini Ram and Malcolm Harper

Routledge
Taylor & Francis Group

LONDON AND NEW YORK

First published 2021
by Routledge
2 Park Square, Milton Park, Abingdon, Oxon OX14 4RN

and by Routledge
52 Vanderbilt Avenue, New York, NY 10017

Routledge is an imprint of the Taylor & Francis Group, an informa business

© 2021 Padmini Ram and Malcolm Harper

The right of Padmini Ram and Malcolm Harper to be identified as authors of this work has been asserted by them in accordance with sections 77 and 78 of the Copyright, Designs and Patents Act 1988.

British Library Cataloguing-in-Publication Data
A catalogue record for this book is available from the British Library

Library of Congress Cataloging-in-Publication Data
A catalog record for this book has been requested

ISBN: 978-1-138-38458-3 (hbk)
ISBN: 978-1-003-09558-3 (ebk)

Typeset in Sabon
by Apex CoVantage, LLC

WE ARE THANKFUL ALSO TO OUR
FAMILIES, WHO WERE GENEROUS WITH
THEIR LOVE AND ENCOURAGEMENT.

TO ASHOK, KUNAL, AND USCHI, WHOSE
WISE COUNSEL HAS ALWAYS SERVED
US WELL.

CONTENTS

FIGURES

TABLES

PREFACE

India is the fifth largest economy in the world; its total wealth as conventionally measured has recently overtaken that of the United Kingdom, and its people's income per head, even when corrected for purchasing power, stands at number 116 out of 179 countries – well ahead of Bolivia and of most countries in Africa, and at a similar level to Morocco or Jamaica. However, by one measure of well-being – or rather 'ill-being', or poverty – India is by far the world's leader. Some 150 million of its population live in slums. This is in spite of successive governments' attempts to overcome the problem – massive subsidies have been poured into attempts to improve the situation, and there has been an almost endless succession of institutions, regulations, and other attempts to remove or even to significantly alleviate what is a national and even an international source of shame. Even now, the number of Indian people living in slums is increasing every day.

We are not, by any means, the first to try to understand the reasons for this sorry state of affairs, or to search for possible remedies, but we have taken what we believe is a rather unusual approach. Our focus has not been on Mumbai, or Kolkata, or on any of the more familiar urban areas which are famous for their slums, which have themselves been recognised and almost celebrated in books and films, but on a relatively unfamiliar city called Raipur.

Raipur is the capital city of the new state called Chhattisgarh, which is itself probably not well known outside India. It was carved out of the state of Madhya Pradesh in the year 2000. Raipur itself has a population of a little over 1 million people, and the city has of course grown a great deal since it became a state capital. Its slums are therefore a rather new phenomenon and cannot be blamed on a long history of urban mismanagement. The slums are young, like the state and city itself. Chhattisgarh was also one of the only states in India to have completely privatised the housing sector for a brief period of time. That was followed by a set of many experiments to promote affordable housing.

Raipur was chosen not only for this reason, but also because it happens to be the hometown of Padmini, one of the two co-authors. Our study was originally undertaken for Padmini's doctoral dissertation at the University of Cambridge in the United Kingdom. Malcolm, the other co-author, was her external examiner at the time. He was impressed by the work, in particular by its practical approach to a problem with which he was very familiar from work elsewhere in India, and to its solution. After a successful examination, he told Padmini that she should be sure to develop the work and publish it, not merely for the sake of her personal academic credit but because of the practical value of her findings and their potential contribution to the improvement of the living conditions of India's millions of slum dwellers.

Padmini approved of the idea, but she insisted that Malcolm should agree to be her co-author, to which he agreed. The book is the result of this collaboration.

ACKNOWLEDGEMENTS

We are indebted to many people without whose help this book might not have been written. Professors Ian Hodge and Phil Allmendinger from Cambridge University provided useful comments for the original doctoral thesis, Professor Needham was also always available to advise and assist, and Professor Peter Tyler, Dr Sarah Monk, and Dr Maria Abreu gave many helpful comments.

We must also thank our fieldwork guide, Sheetal Tandi, and all the interviewees and survey participants. The project management unit of the Jawaharlal Nehru National Urban Renewal Mission in Raipur kindly provided office space and also helped with fieldwork logistics. Special thanks to the staff there – Archana Bondriya, Komal Bhalla, Anand Deheria, Rana Thakur, and our driver, Ganesh.

The original doctoral research was only possible because of financial support and scholarship grants from the Cambridge Political Economy Society, the Cambridge University Graduate Student Research Scheme, the Clare Hall Research Scholarship, the Smut's Memorial travel grant, and the Gilchrist Educational Trust.

Thanks to all of them, from both of us – and, we hope, from the millions of less well-off Indian slum dwellers whose living conditions will eventually improve in part as a result of our work.

1

THE AFFORDABLE HOUSING PUZZLE

About 150 million people live in slums in India (Jain, Chennuri, & Karam-chandani, 2016), more than the whole population of countries such as Russia, Mexico, and Japan. India is rapidly becoming richer, and although it is still home to far more poor people than any other country, the proportion of its people who are desperately poor is going down quite fast.

Nevertheless, the slum population continues to grow; this book analyses the situation of slum dwellers, the problems they face, the incomes they earn, and the reasons why they have to live in slums. The study whose results it describes was carried out in Raipur, a rapidly growing city in central India with a population of over a million people, which is typical of urban India.

We also propose some remedies that we believe to be practical, fairly simple, and inexpensive. We hope that our findings can help towards the solution of what is surely one of the most deplorable but nevertheless the most remediable problems facing India, and the world as a whole.

This introductory chapter starts with some short case studies describing people whom we met. These cases are followed by a more detailed analysis of the current situation and the reasons for it, including the constraints to supply and effective demand. The book ends with some recommendations which will, we hope, be of practical value to all the different agencies whose cooperation will be needed if the present appalling situation is to be addressed effectively.

Case 1 – Rukmani and Dukhiram: the aspirational couple

Rukmani works as domestic help for six families who live near her home, which is in a slum in Gandhi Nagar, Raipur.[1] She earns approximately Rs. 2000, or 27 USD, from each family – or about Rs. 12,000, or 160 USD, per month. Her husband is a mason who learnt the trade on the job. Nowadays he likes to call himself a *thekedar*, or contractor, because he takes up petty jobs on a contractual basis. Between them, they earned around Rs. 25,000–30,000, or between 350 USD and 400 USD, per month in 2012. They are migrants to the city; Rukmani's parents live in Dhamtari, about

80 kilometres away, and Dukhiram, her husband, is a member of the Gond tribe, whose village is around 250 kilometres away. His father is a highly regarded elder in the village, and his brother is a village headman or *sarpanch*. They have three children.

Their two-room house is what is called *pucca*, meaning it is built of brick and mortar and has a reinforced cement concrete (RCC) roof. They built the house themselves on a 600-square-foot space in the slum. They are squatters and have no legal right to the site but have occupied it for the last 20 years. As of January 2012, they had already spent nearly Rs. 75,000, or over 1000 USD, on building the house, not including Dukhiram's labour. The day I visited them in their house, Dukhiram was tiling the bathroom walls. Rukmani was very proud to show off their new home that was under construction, and they were already living in it. They had been building it for over two years and they added new extensions, such as the first floor of the home, as and when they had been able to save enough money for the materials. Dukhiram's work meant that they spent no money on labour. Rukmani was optimistic that by the end of October 2012, they would be able to paint the walls and add the final touches to the building. Although they had no title to the house, as required by a Supreme Court ruling, the State Electricity Board had provided them with an electricity connection, and the municipality had provided a water connection. They had a television, their own mobile phones, an internet cable connection, and a cooler for use during the summer months. The slum is in a low-lying area of the city and can be flooded during the monsoon (rainy season).

Case 2 – Devaki's large extended family

Devaki is a young woman from a tribe in the neighbouring state of Odisha. She works as a cook and domestic helper in several houses in and around the area where she lives. She is heavily pregnant, so her younger sister-in-law, Sudha, works in her place to keep the job. Sudha goes in early as she attends school during the day, and she also works after her school is over in the afternoon. Devaki's father-in-law migrated to Raipur 40 years ago. He was one of the first squatters on the railway land beside the Raipur–Dhamtari line. Devaki's husband has no regular work, but their joint family is doing reasonably well. They say that their family income is around Rs. 100,000, or 1350 USD, per month. Her father-in-law owns a small grocery store whose customers are mostly fellow residents of the slum. Their house has 9 rooms, including the one which is used as a shop. They 'own' four other houses in the slum. In their slum, squatting rights for a small, one-room hut are sold by 'owners' such as Devaki's father-in-law for over half a million rupees, almost 6700 USD, or rented for Rs. 800 (10 USD) per month. Devaki's brother-in-law serves local snacks in the early mornings from a pushcart near their house on the main road. Later in the morning, he sells cheap tobacco products and mouth fresheners from the same pushcart. The family has an electric power connection and tap water. They also have a television, several mobile phones, and air coolers for the Raipur summers when temperatures can go up to 46° C (114° F). But they live in fear of eviction, as many of their neighbours have received notices to vacate their plots.

Case 3 – Lakshmi: the single mother

Lakshmi is a single mother who was deserted by her husband within a year of her marriage. She lives with her 15-year-old daughter in a hut beside the railway line. She rents the hut for Rs. 800 per month, although the 'owner' has no title over the property. Lakshmi works as an office cleaner in a few offices and as a domestic worker for various clients and earns a total of about Rs. 6000, or 80 USD, per month.

Case 4 – Sushil: the young migrant

Sushil is an office boy during the day and sleeps as a watchman during the night in a garage, a portion of which also serves as his 'house'. The garage is about 10 kilometres away from the office where he works. He cycles to work, so his travel does not cost him anything. He earns Rs. 7000, or around 95 USD, per month from the office, and he pays no rent for his 'accommodation'. This helps him save for his future. He is planning to get married once he has saved enough and can find a proper house.

Case 5 – Mathura: the family's breadwinner

Mathura is a domestic worker. She works for several different people and earns around Rs. 12,000, or 160 USD, per month. Her husband is a watch-man who works for the government forest department on an urban social-forestry project for about Rs. 6,000 or 80 USD per month. The project never took off properly, but Mathura's husband was allowed to live rent-free in a hut on the project land. They have electricity and water connections but may be evicted at any time because her husband may lose his job. He is looking for an alternative, more lucrative job, such as selling at one of the shops in the nearby mall. This would not require any formal education and would pay about Rs. 12,000, or 160 USD, per month.

Case 6 – The typical coexisting family with multiple incomes

Sheetal Tandi was our field assistant from January–September 2012. She lived in a slum and was recruited because she seemed to be lively, outgoing, and resourceful. She is 15 years old and studies in the local government school and works part-time as domestic help. She is the youngest of her parents' five children, and they all live together in a three-room house. Her mother also works as domestic help, and her father pedals a rickshaw.

Her brother is a sales assistant in a shop in a nearby mall; her oldest sister works in a bank, another sister works in a beauty parlour, and the third sister is training to be a nurse and works part-time in a hospital. The father earns the least and spends most of his income on alcohol, although he took good care of the family when they were young. As the children grew older and started working, the family has become better off. They save most of their earnings and spend very little on maintaining the house, but they plan to renovate it for the oldest sister's wedding. She makes all the major decisions at home and said that the family's income is about Rs. 50,000, or almost 700 USD, per month. Sheetal said that this cannot be considered as 'family income' because the sisters and the brother do not share all of their money. But when she was asked who will pay for the renovation, she answered, "everyone will chip in".

These few cases are typical of the sample of 211 families from Raipur's slums who were interviewed for the study on which this book is based. Raipur is the capital of Chhattisgarh, which was carved out of the state of Madhya Pradesh in central India in November 2000. It is the tenth-largest state by area. Chhattisgarh began with great promise, blessed with natural resources including iron ore, coal, bauxite, and limestone; nearly 40% forest cover; several rivers that helped win for the State the epithet of the "rice bowl of India"; and surplus electric power. Raipur became the state's capital and was soon a bustling business centre. Chhattisgarh witnessed considerable foreign direct investment.

Chhattisgarh presents an interesting case for this study, as it is the only state in India to have completely privatised the housing sector. When this failed to create the desired market, public provision of affordable housing was reinstated. The State privatised the housing sector and disbanded the state Housing Board in 2002 to stop what was seen as market distortion and to allow private builders to service the demand (see Chapter 2). However, the private builders who invested in housing catered to higher incomes, ignoring the greater numbers of lower incomes. The result was a surplus of higher-priced housing while affordable housing was in acute short supply.

A report (2007) published by Chhattisgarh Housing Board acknowledges this:

> "Private sector builders receive full encouragement from the Government. However, it was observed that the private sector, driven by concerns for return on investment, focuses on the top-end of the housing market. They have little or no interest in the low end."

CHHATTISGARH

GEOGRAPHICAL SCOPE
CHHATTISGARH

Formed in November 2000, 10th largest state of India by area (135,192 km sq or 52,198 sq mi), population 2011: 2.56 Crores (25.6 million)

URBAN CENTRE: RAIPUR

Centre of the fieldwork area

226 km sq (87 sq mi), population– Raipur (Municipal Corporation) approx 100,000 (1 million) according to Census 2011

Figure 1.1 Geographical scope of Chhattisgarh

Source: Shutterstock

Disclaimer: The international boundaries, coastlines, denominations, and other information shown in any map in this work do not necessarily imply any judgement concerning the legal status of any territory or the endorsement or acceptance of such information. For current boundaries, readers may refer to the Survey of India maps.

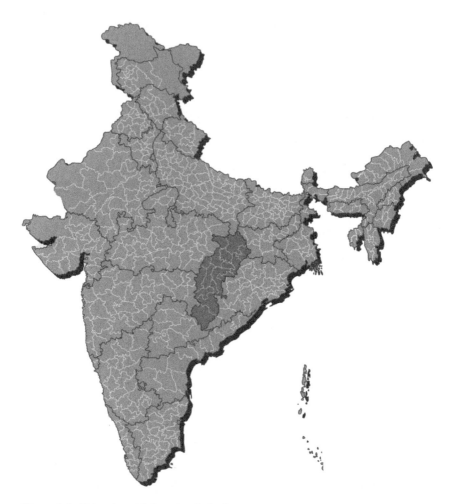

Figure 1.2 Chhattisgarh's location in India
Source: Shutterstock

In 2004 the government of Chhattisgarh, realizing the gravity of the problem regarding affordable housing, re-created the Chhattisgarh Housing Board to focus on the housing needs of the urban poor. The Chhattisgarh Housing Board (2007) claims to have created more affordable housing stock in three years than was created in the region in the preceding 30 years. Since 2008, the Chhattisgarh Housing Board (CGHB) has won several national awards for its performance. However, the housing stock remains grossly inadequate.

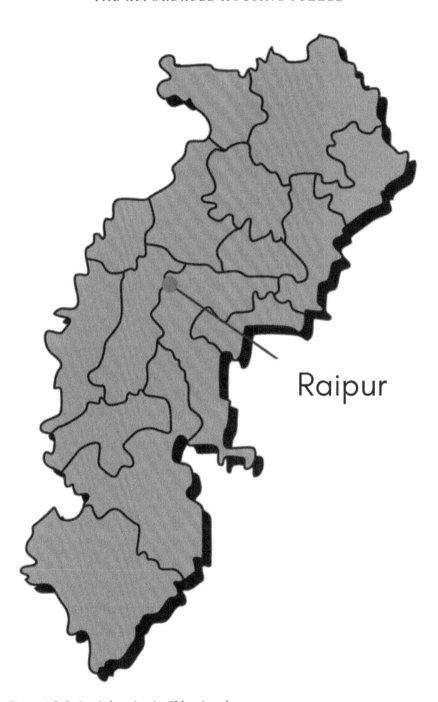

Figure 1.3 Raipur's location in Chhattisgarh
Source: Shutterstock

Most of these housing experiments took place in Raipur and impacted this city the most.

In Chhattisgarh, the housing shortage in urban areas is higher than in rural areas, unlike the situation in India as a whole (Table 1.1). A Government of India (GoI) committee report (2012) estimated the housing shortage in Chhattisgarh (in 2012) to be around 0.35 million in the urban areas alone. According to the 2011 census, the slum population of Chhattisgarh was 1,900,000, and in Raipur it was around 0.37 million. With almost 39% of its urban population living in slums, Raipur is listed among the top ten cities in India having a population over a million with a high proportion of slum households (Census, 2011).

Although the CGHB was reinstated, the state is aware that it does not have the resources to continue to subsidise housing in this way. Hence, in 2004, the state government of Chhattisgarh (GoCG) came up with a state housing policy along the lines of the national housing policy, seeking private sector participation. However, this did not make a significant impact on increasing private sector involvement in affordable housing (CGHB, 2007). A shortage of affordable housing led to the mushrooming of slums. Chhattisgarh is also among the three states that have the highest percentage of slum households to total urban households.

The slums differ in geographical location, and therefore in their access to various amenities. Though most slums have mixed groups, some slums are divided on the lines of occupation, such as the ironsmiths in *Loharpara*; by regional communities defined by where they migrated from, like Orissa or Madhya Pradesh; or are local *Chattisgarhias*, as people from the same caste tend to reside together. To reduce the anomalous effects of such systematic differences, the data was collected through random sampling from households belonging to 19 different slums spread across 16 wards of the Raipur Municipal Corporation area, covering all eight zones.

For the sampling, every third or fourth door depending on the size of the slum was selected, starting with the house of the person who was introducing us to the slum. The neighbours living on their street could be convinced

Table 1.1 Housing shortage (in millions) in India and Chhattisgarh

Census 2001				In 2007	In 2012
	Rural	Urban	Total	Urban	Urban
Chhattisgarh	0.02	0.08	0.10	0.36	0.35
India	14.12	10.56	24.68	24.71	18.78
Source: (National Housing Bank, 2006)				(MoHUPA, NBO, GoI, 2012)	(MoHUPA, NBO, GoI, 2012)

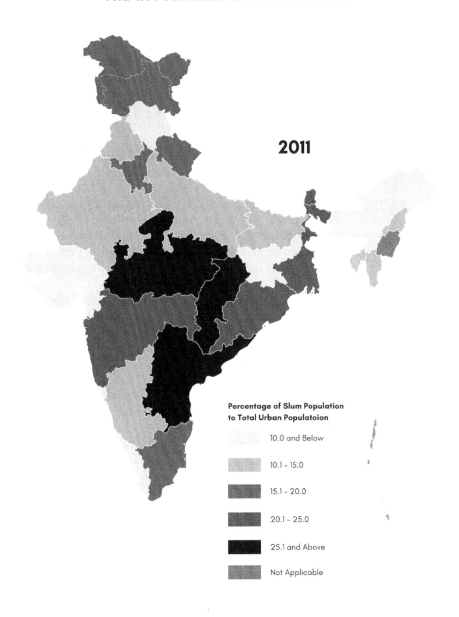

Figure 1.4 Percentage of slum households to total urban households (census 2011)
Source: Chandramouli (2011)

more easily; hence, it always served as the starting point. If the next randomly selected house was locked or the residents did not wish to or were incapable of responding, such as elderly parents or teenage children who were unaware of the family finances, or earned more than the income range considered by the study, then the next house was selected, and then every third or fourth door from there on. Approximately 20% of the households in the surveyed slums earned more than the income range considered by the study and were therefore not included.

The official categorisation for people whose annual household income is under Rs. 100,000 (1350 USD) per annum is 'economically weaker sections' (EWS), and for those between Rs. 100,001 – Rs. 200,000 (1350–2700 USD) per annum the categorisation is Low Income Group (LIG). In this book, we use the terms 'very poor' and 'poor' instead of the acronyms. Together, they constitute the urban poor. The interviews were carried out in 2012; however, land, labour, and other costs have remained in approximately the same relationship to the earnings of the various income groups.

People in the slums tended to understate their earnings. Some of the poor households would, at the beginning of the survey, categorise themselves as very poor, but with more questions would reveal that they earned a lot more. They were especially unwilling to share information about any additional homes or land that they might have elsewhere. A majority were of the opinion that only those who were rendered homeless in case of slum clearance, because they had no second home, would be entitled to free homes. As a result, they were apprehensive about sharing such information, even if it was for academic purposes.

Around 70% were self-employed – small shopkeepers and restaurant owners, drivers, wedding band musicians, *halwai* who cook for large events such as weddings and other social functions, mechanics, blacksmiths, handymen and plumbers, masons, barbers and salon owners, laundrymen, street vendors, and brokers, who arrange weddings, land and vehicle deals, and settle disputes, all for a fee.

About 30% of the families who were interviewed were salaried employees, working for private and government employers. They included cashiers, drivers, security personnel, beauticians, and shop workers, while those in the public sector worked in the police, in the health department, and for the railways. Fifty-five percent of those who were interviewed, or 116 households, were casual labourers; they worked as domestic help, rickshaw pullers, auto-rickshaw drivers, or construction workers.

Although all the families described in these short case studies lived in the slums, they had the means to afford a decent living. They were also willing to pay for it. Our findings revealed that 80% of the 211 households were able to afford decent formal housing. That is, they could have afforded the down payment and the monthly instalment for a mortgage at commercial interest rates to cover the full cost of such housing, with secure titles. This seemed to go against the common idea we have about slum dwellers. If they actually can afford it, why have they not acquired proper houses? Why do they continue to live in appalling conditions and without any legally secure tenure? When they were asked these questions, the answer was obvious: Such housing is not available. The largest provider of affordable housing is the State – or more precisely, the Chhattisgarh Housing Board.

However, the supply is too small for the demand. About 125,000 households live in slums in Raipur, but since 2004, government agencies have been able to build no more than 5000 dwellings per year in Raipur (Interviewee-3F). At this rate, it would take 25 years to re-house all the slum households in the city even if the population were to remain constant. The situation is similar or worse elsewhere in India. In Kolkata, for example, government agencies produce on average about 500 dwellings per year. This constitutes less than 1% of the city's yearly housing need (Sengupta & Tipple, 2007).

Can this unmet demand be serviced by private developers? Or is the price that slum dwellers can afford too low for private developers to be interested?

There are about 70 developers operating in Raipur. Thirty randomly selected developers were interviewed to find out whether it was technically and economically possible to build houses for a price that slum dwellers could afford. If it was possible, what was stopping the developers from building such housing?

The results of these 30 interviews were surprising. The developers were aware of the market potential for affordable housing but that had no control over the number of houses which were built in the "affordable housing" sector; the Government calls for bids after acquiring land through the process of land acquisition. The developers build the houses on contract to the Government. They are allowed a fixed 10% "profit" on their work, and the houses have to be built as per the current regulations.

There seemed to be no reason why the same builders could not build houses of the same quality, for the same cost, including the price of land, and could then sell them on the open market to the present slum dwellers whose incomes are sufficient to pay the full market cost. It appeared, in addition, that the current rules caused the cost of so-called 'low-cost housing' to be about one-third more than it needed to be. Simple changes to some of these rules could make the houses even more affordable, without reducing the builders' 10% profit.

This book is a hopeful account of a feasible solution to the affordable housing problem. Although the study was carried out in Raipur, it tells an Indian story. The 37 million urban Indian families who live in informal housing are occupying land which is in theory illegally occupied, and their unplanned settlements usually lack basic infrastructure and services. By no means, however, are all of these people destitute or unemployed vagrants. Most of them are ordinary working people who work in the informal and formal economy, earn decent cash incomes, and share the same aspirations as the rest of us, including to live in decent housing. Most slum dwellers, however, are prevented from converting their ability and willingness to spend into genuine demand. This book attempts to identify the constraints and to suggest ways in which they can be overcome.

Note

1 All names of respondents in this book have been changed and/or anonymised.

2

THE STORY SO FAR

What is happening in global housing policy?

Ensuring decent housing for all has been a challenge that has attracted researchers and practitioners from various fields. The topics range from the technical aspects such as financing mechanisms, construction practices, design and building techniques, and planning permits, to cultural and social issues such as cohesion, community and citizen participation, environment and its impact on health, human settlements, and liveable cities.

Unarguably, there are some best practices that have emerged over the years. Outlining some of those experiences would be a good first step in the search for strategies appropriate to the situation in India. However, it is not an easy task. To begin with, there is no consensus about what can be considered "affordable housing". For example, can a dwelling in a squatter settlement be called affordable housing? After all, as the term suggests, it is affordable. Some view the informal sector as a way of fulfilling the shelter needs of a particular group. Informal housing markets are, in that sense, a market response to the institutional constraints in the low-income housing sector in terms of their "ability to deliver according to the economic capacities of the poor" better than the formal sector.

This was the stance based on the works of Charles Abrams (1964, 1966) and John Turner (1968), who viewed squatter settlements and the self-help initiatives of the poor as a solution to housing problems. The assumption was if the slum inhabitants were capable of building their dwellings under adverse conditions, they would do much better with the government's support.

There have been serious debates on whether the provision should be through formal or informal mechanisms, and on who should be the provider – market or state, or maybe a non-governmental organisation (NGO) or a public–private partnership.

There are advantages and disadvantages in every kind of provision – informal practices are generally faster and more price sensitive to the paying capacity of the poor. Similarly, even among formal approaches, market mechanisms are definitely faster, and often provide a greater choice to consumers than public housing. On the other hand, even with longer waiting periods, public housing is often subsidised or rent controlled. In most cases, unlike dwellings in squatter settlements, it ensures access to five basic amenities: drinking water, toilets, electricity, drainage, and roads.

Berner (2000) points out that reasonable criticism of the formal system should not lead to a romanticised view of informal institutions. Informal housing solutions do not offer adequate security or any insurance against the innumerable and constant risks that the people are living in. Marcuse (1992) adds that they can provide only marginally, inefficiently, and exploitatively, as disorganised habitation leads to inefficient use of land and cannot deal with a host of problems that require centralised decision making; they violate sound and necessary planning principles. Therefore, they are likely to produce only temporary solutions to immediate housing problems. They also limit capital accumulation and growth (De Soto, 2000). We therefore argue that it is desirable to stimulate a formal housing market for the urban poor. This is not to say that informal housing does not have its benefits.

We begin by surveying some of the best practices in the formal approaches to the provision of affordable housing. To accommodate several practices, we have defined the term very broadly in this review. It is commonly understood as shelter provided to specified eligible households whose needs are not met by the market. The government provides it either on its own or through NGOs and other funding agencies. It includes various kinds of housing provision, each with its own eligibility criteria meeting different needs, which collectively form a housing continuum illustrated in Figure 2.1.

Some of the commonly used housing policies and/or practices are detailed in the following section. This is by no means exhaustive. Selected "best practices" from Asia and affordable housing provisions in the United States (US) and United Kingdom (UK) are presented.

Types of affordable housing initiatives, globally

Transitional shelters (emergency and night shelters, transitional homes, and working women's hostels)

Emergency shelters are provided by the government (often with the help of relief organisations such as the International Red Cross) in emergencies such as fire, floods, or natural disasters such as hurricanes or cyclones. Night shelters provide free basic accommodation during the coldest winter months. Many are run by faith groups or charities, but they serve anyone who visits the shelter. Transitional housing programmes are more common in developed countries such as the US and UK and provide temporary residence for

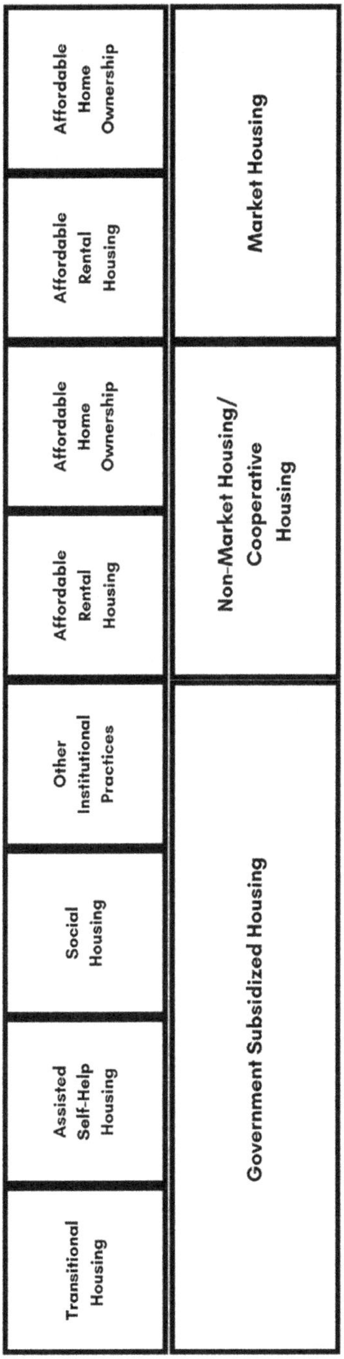

Transitional Housing	Assisted Self-Help Housing	Social Housing	Other Institutional Practices	Affordable Rental Housing	Affordable Home Ownership	Affordable Rental Housing	Affordable Home Ownership
Government Subsidized Housing				Non-Market Housing/ Cooperative Housing		Market Housing	

Figure 2.1 The affordable housing continuum

Source: Authors' construction

15

people experiencing homelessness due to factors such as domestic violence or drug abuse. Housing is combined with other services to assist individuals in developing stability in their lives.

The Working Women's hostel is a popular form of shelter in India. It started with the Young Women's Christian Association (YWCA) movement in India, housing young working women away from home. It remains a much-needed service for women of all categories. In 1972–1973, the government of India introduced a Scheme for Working Women, which provided grants for construction of new buildings or expansion of existing buildings for providing hostel facilities to working women in urban and some rural areas. A number of NGOs operate such hostels.

Assisted self-help housing

While the self-help paradigm has dominated housing policy discourse, actual housing sector practice in terms of what constitutes "self-help" has been extremely diverse. Programmes such as the Kampung Improvement Programme in Indonesia, the Baan Mankong Programme in Thailand, and Indiramma Yojna in India aim to work with the residents by providing building materials, loans, and technical support to upgrade their existing dwellings. The land is either regularised or made available through a long-term lease, cooperative land ownership, or distribution of land titles. It also offers the opportunity to upskill the community by forming small building groups, cooperatives, or mason training. In some ways, it is similar to the incremental self-build programmes promoted by Slum Dwellers International.

Often, NGOs are the principal actors in assisted self-help housing, by organizing potential beneficiaries into community groups, informing them of their rights, lobbying for government assistance, and sometimes even acting as the developer of the infrastructure and dwellings. Habitat for Humanity (HfH), Practical Action (PA), National Slum Dwellers Federation (NSDF), and the Society for the Promotion of Area Resource Centers (SPARC) are some of the NGOs working in the affordable housing sector.

These programmes have used innovative approaches based on principles of inclusive zoning and transfer of development rights (TDR). One such example, from the Dharavi slum in Mumbai, has been documented by Sanyal and Mukhija (2001). The state government wanted to redevelop Dharavi but also minimise the relocation of slum inhabitants, encouraging them to contribute financially towards the project cost and to work with cooperative housing societies responsible for design, construction, and maintenance of the property. It was led by the NGO SPARC, together with NSDF and the Mahila Milan (MM). SPARC has a division called Samudaya Nirman Sahayak (SSNS), a sister NGO that assists communities with financial and technical aspects of housing development and construction.

The municipality leased the land to the cooperative, which then used the lease as collateral to raise funds. The government provided 15% of the project cost and a 20% interest-free loan. Housing finance loans made up 50% of the cost, and the balance was contributed by the beneficiaries. The existing slum dwellers were provided with cooperatively owned, multi-storey accommodations with legal tenure.

However, after several issues and years of conflict, the final project that evolved was in-situ reconstruction, whereby private developers as well as housing cooperatives could be promoters in redeveloping slums. The eligible slum dwellers received housing units of 17–21 square metres and did not pay more than 23% of the cost. Building and selling additional units at market price to high-income buyers generated enough profit to cross-subsidise the slumdwellers. The government increased the floor-to-area ratio (FAR) for the project and allowed TDR benefit to the builder so that he could partially transfer the development rights to other high-priced areas in the city, thereby providing him with a greater incentive to rebuild in the poor areas.

Based on similar principles, the Community-led Infrastructure Finance Facility (CLIFF) by Homeless International supported 15 projects in India by providing loan finance for slum development. One such project was operated in conjunction with SPARC and SSNS, which includes the construction of over 5300 new homes.

While many such processes of self-build and bottom-up development have come up, they do not provide a sufficiently fast or large-scale solution to the immense housing demand facing Asian cities (UN-HABITAT, 2011).

Social housing

In Southeast Asia, Singapore and Hong Kong have developed a number of subsidised public housing programmes, reportedly resulting in almost universal access to adequate housing. Their success is attributed to centralised governments with highly regulated economies, steady economic growth, lack of rural migrants, and the availability of publicly owned land with appropriately regulated land policies. In other Asian countries, however, direct public housing provision has had very limited success (UN-HABITAT, 2011).

THE UNITED STATES

There are several affordable housing schemes in the United States, most of which provide grants to fund building, buying, and/or rehabilitating housing for rent or homeownership or provide direct rental assistance to low-income families. The HOME Investment Partnerships Program is the largest federal block grant programme for state and local governments designed exclusively to create affordable housing. The National Housing Trust Fund supports families with incomes below the poverty line. The Self-Help

Homeownership Opportunity Program (SHOP) provides funds for non-profit organisations to purchase home sites for low-income families and to develop or improve the infrastructure for sweat equity and volunteer-based homeownership programmes. The US Department of Housing and Urban Development (HUD) also helps apartment owners offer reduced rents to low-income tenants under its privately owned subsidised housing scheme, and to the elderly and persons with disabilities under the public housing scheme. Apart from these schemes, the Housing Choice Voucher Program provides demand-side subsidies for housing (HUD, 2015).

THE UNITED KINGDOM

Qualifying households in the United Kingdom join the local authority's waiting list or housing register, where a points or banding system determines the applicant's priority (Shelter UK, 2015a). Social affordable housing is largely rental, with an option or right to buy in certain cases. It has various types of tenancies, each having its set of rights and responsibilities. New tenants are usually offered a starter tenancy, such as a 'trial' period of twelve months, which may then be converted to an assured or fixed term. An assured tenancy normally allows people to live in the property indefinitely, while a fixed-term tenancy is for at least five years, with the landlord having the discretion for renewal (ibid.).

The British government has also created a range of Help to Buy products, such as Shared Ownership and Equity loans. Shared Ownership allows the purchase of a percentage share of a property while paying a subsidised rent on the remaining share. Further shares can be bought until the property is owned outright. Under the Equity Loan scheme, one can purchase specific new-build properties, where the government lends 20% of the cost so that homebuyers need to provide only a 5% cash deposit and can thus secure a 75% mortgage. The loan fee is waived on the 20% loan for the first five years of ownership (Help to buy, 2015). In spite of these programmes, 5000 or so people sleep on the streets in the UK every night; this is less than 0.01% of the total population, but the figure nevertheless demonstrates that housing for all is difficult to achieve, even in a wealthy 'developed' economy.

Other institutional practices for affordable housing

Land

Support from the public sector is crucial for securing land for affordable housing. Needham and de Kam (2000) have categorised such support under the following six approaches:

- reserving land for social housing to avoid competition;
- subsidising the acquisition of land;

- subsidising construction costs to make more money available for land;
- subsidising tenants so they can pay higher rents, which increases the amount that providers can offer for the land; and
- subsidising the purchase costs when the housing is for sale.

In China, urban land belongs to the state. The government leases the land to developers through an auction, to construct affordable housing which is sold to people in need. The government provides low-income households with one-off equity grants, and developers are offered fiscal incentives to build housing within a negotiated price range. More than 20 million dwellings were constructed through this approach in a five-year period (UN-HABITAT, 2011).

Mortgage

There is a range of innovative approaches to housing finance throughout Asia, such as government subsidies in China and India, or community-led initiatives such as the Community Mortgage Programme in the Philippines and the Grameen Bank's micro credit. Singapore's Central Provident Fund (CPF) helps households to save by contributing a certain percentage of their monthly income to a tax-exempt housing fund. Ninety-five percent of employees aged 21 and above own public housing brought with CPF savings (UN-HABITAT, 2011).

Islamic housing finance (Musharakah) in Pakistan works on a declining-balance or shared-equity partnership, where the bank buys the house and leases it back to the consumer. The consumer then buys units of the property and eventually buys out the financiers' equity and acquires an individual title. This approach is less risky for the bank and reduces the down payment requirement, which is often the main barrier to securing housing finance (Askaribank, 2015). This model applies to all sections of society, and it is not clear what proportion is available to poorer people.

Non-market housing/cooperative housing/public–private partnerships

Non-market housing

Non-market housing includes provision by private providers through conditions placed on planning permission for housing development. Various state governments in India, such as Chhattisgarh and Haryana, require that developers reserve a certain percentage of the total plots or number of dwellings that they develop for urban poor families. Similarly, other states such as Maharashtra permit a 20% increase in the normally permissible density limits for schemes where at least 60% of the dwellings are reserved for the urban poor. Such practices are common in other countries as well.

Cooperative housing

Housing cooperatives exist in various forms throughout North America, Southeast Asia, and Europe, and have effectively built and managed affordable housing since the 1900s. Cooperatives promote long-term affordability primarily through agreed limits on resale prices of shares. Income restrictions on buyers of affordable housing cooperative shares ensure that the housing remains targeted to those who need it (CMHN & VNC, 2004).

A housing cooperative is a legal and usually non-profit corporation which owns or leases all its real estate. The occupants have to buy or rent shares to obtain membership in a cooperative, which grants an exclusive right to live in a specific unit for as long as the occupant wishes and adheres to the cooperative's rules and regulations.

Members set the bylaws and elect, from among themselves, a board of directors. The board organises a membership meeting at least annually and hires staff to run the day-to-day business of the cooperative, such as maintenance, landscaping, handling finances, and organizing social activities. As part of the membership, the occupant has a vote in the corporation's affairs. At-cost operations, personal income tax deductions, less frequent ownership changes, lower real estate tax assessments in some local areas, and well-controlled maintenance costs make cooperative housing more affordable than regular private housing (Sliogeris, Crabtree, Phibbs, Johnston, & O'Neill, 2008; NCDF, n.d.; NAHC, 2015).

Public–Private Partnership (PPP) models

Within India, Kolkata pioneered the implementation of the PPP model, based on a joint venture model. The equity shares of public partners range between 11% and 49.5%, depending upon the social value of the project. By 2004, 3554 units were transferred to the public since the policy's implementation in 1993, and 3000 additional units were under construction, which equates to an average annual production of roughly 500 dwellings. The overall output constitutes less than 1% of the city's yearly average housing need (UN-HABITAT, 2011; Sengupta & Tipple, 2007).

Shortage of affordable housing persists

Despite these programmes, the shortage of affordable housing persists in most countries. Even in wealthier countries, especially in cities such as London and New York City, there is an acute shortage of affordable housing. More than 88,000 people applied for one offer of 55 low-cost units in New York City (Navarro, 2015). One in four renter households in the United States pays more than half their income on rent, and another 610,000 people or 400,000 households were stated to be "homeless" in 2013. Over 18 million low-income families across the United States, including 10.9 million who were renting their homes and 7.5 million homeowners, are said to be "cost burdened" – meaning that they pay more than half their income on housing. Many believe that the affordable housing issue may be under-stated, as the housing industry lacks complete data on all forms of housing instability – especially households that miss rent payments, move involun-tarily, or share their homes because they cannot afford to live on their own (Enterprise Community Partners, 2014).

The problem is worse in Asia because of the unprecedented pace of urban-isation, with around 44 million more people being added to the continent's city population every year. This growth requires the construction of more than 20,000 new dwellings every day (UN-HABITAT, 2011). It is a major challenge to provide affordable housing at the required pace and scale, and at the same time for the programmes to be financially sustainable for both governments and non-profit organisations in the housing sector.

An enabling strategy for a formal affordable housing market, internationally

On 20 December 1988, the UN General Assembly adopted a resolution (A/RES/43/181) on Global Strategy for Shelter to the Year 2000, which pro-vided guidelines for steps to be taken at the national level and outlined the considerations for governments when formulating a national shelter strat-egy. The launch of the Global Shelter Strategy (GSS) in 1988 introduced the *enabling strategy* into many national housing policies. Prior to the first Hab-itat Conference in 1976, there were no global initiatives on housing policy. The national governments formulated and implemented their own housing policies and strategies, often by copying European examples of public hous-ing which could not provide a fraction of what was needed, and most of the houses constructed were built only for government employees. Slum clear-ance in the Western style has been the major response in many developing countries in dealing with squatter settlements (UN-Habitat, 2003).

The GSS based on the works of Charles Abrams (1964, 1966) and John Turner (1968) provided an alternative, more positive view of slums and squatter settlements. They did not subscribe to the earlier view that these were places of filth and crime, which needed "slum clearing". They argued that governments are clearly incapable of financing housing for all. It was, therefore, irrational to destroy what little the slum dwellers had accumu-lated and built on their own. Rather, if the governments supported these efforts, the slum dwellers would be able to build better homes.

This view influenced the first global conference on human settlements, which was held in 1976 in Vancouver, Canada. This conference produced an Action Plan with recommendations for enabling shelter strategies at the national level. This marked a major turning point in the evolution of housing policy. The United Nations Centre for Human Settlements (UN-Habitat) was established in 1978 as a follow-up to the 1976 Conference, with a mandate to promote the Vancouver Action Plan and to guide national housing policies around the world (Tipple & Majale, 2006).

The 'sites-and-services' approach was the first formal "global" strategy that replaced both slum clearance and conventional housing for government employees. It turned the focus of global housing strategy on to the housing needs of the poor. The housing agencies were tasked with preparing the land, laying out the streets, and providing trunk infrastructure (World Bank. Office of Environmental Affairs, 1974), while households were expected to incrementally construct their dwellings. These strategies stressed the need for "restoring planning control" (van der Linden, 1986).

However, the first few sites-and-services projects sponsored by the World Bank during the late 1970s turned out to be non-replicable due to high costs and poor project response. The projects which had been supported by international financial institutions were then downscaled. The new approach was termed "slum upgrading", which was considered to be the "alternative that has come to be regarded as best practice in dealing with the problems of squatter slums" (UN-Habitat, 2003). The projects were now mostly in-situ and were taken up in a phased manner, with smaller, more modest projects for water supply and road construction. The biggest difference was that slum upgrading projects were considerably cheaper; it was estimated in 1980 that they cost 38 USD per household, compared to 1000 USD to 2000 USD for a core sites-and-services project (ibid.).

Another important change that led to a reduction in project costs was the form of tenure. The earlier approach had opted for full legalisation of tenure in accordance with the existing land titling laws of the respective countries, but this was very slow and inevitably delayed the progress of projects. Various studies, such as those by Gulyani and Bassett (2007), claimed that there is a distinction between providing security of tenure and issuing land titles, and that provision of infrastructure seemed to provide the slum dwellers with a sense of security sufficient for them to invest in improving properties that they already occupied; time-consuming *de-jure* forms of security were replaced by the more expedient *de-facto* sense of security provided by state-sponsored infrastructure development in the slums.

The focus on land titles has been criticised as leading to distress land sales, resident displacement, or rising rents because of the commodification of squatter land (Payne, 2001a; Hartzok, 2003). However, recent research has pointed out that commodification of land is not dependent on legal titles; even infrastructural fixes in informal housing developments are leading to speculation in slums, which is actually decreasing the security of tenure of the slum residents (Desai & Loftus, 2013; Mukherji & Bharucha, 2011; Rossi, 2011).

Slum upgrading projects yielded mixed results, and in some cases (Majale, 2008; IDB, 2012) there was a vast improvement in housing conditions. However, slum upgrading programmes were often considered a matter of "faking a success" (Verma, 2002). There were also cases where the programmes got 'hijacked', either by the local elite or more frequently by the "foreign philanthropies" working along with the NGOs (Davis, 2007). Critics of slum upgrading programmes characterised some of the NGOs working with the government as the "new class middle-men" (Verma, 2002) pushing their own agendas or acting as "agents of the state" (Zérah, 2009). Verma (2002) presents two celebrated cases of slum upgrading programmes in India, both of which had won several international awards.

The first one was the UK-sponsored Indore scheme, which aimed to provide slum households with individual water and sewer connections. However, a point that was not considered in the programme was that residents did not have enough water to drink, much less to flush waste, so sewage backed up into homes and streets, malaria and cholera spread, and residents began to die from contaminated water (Verma pp 8–15). The second was the Aranya resettlement project; in this case, most of the project's achievements that were being celebrated were literally only on paper, that "a drawing, a design idea" had won awards which no one was sure would work, as it had not been tested (Verma pp 33–35).

That said, both critics and supporters of slum upgrading programmes would agree that in spite of scaling down the slum improvement efforts, governments simply do not have enough resources to support all the slums and their dwellers through even the most basic slum upgrading.

Enabling housing markets

An alternative to slum upgrading but part of the "enabling" approach was the enabling markets strategy. The World Bank suggested the *Enabling Market Strategy*, based on privatisation, deregulation, and decentralisation (The World Bank, 1991, 1993). This implied creating conditions, institutions, and regulations aimed at supporting housing finance systems to promote home ownership, under neo-liberal principles of reliance on private property and market forces.

These neo-liberal economic policies were based on the failure of the government to improve access to housing and other urban facilities (The World Bank, 1997). The idea was that free market mechanisms were better able to deliver, even to the lower strata of the society, and would bring more economic advancement than a regulated economy. Therefore, the economic role of the state should be minimised, leaving the price mechanism in competitive markets to take care of the dynamics of growth and development of backward economies (Sandhu & Korzeniewski, 2004).

To bolster the demand for privately produced residential units, governments shifted their focus from supply-side to demand-side subsidies. Programmes were designed with the rationale that low-income households would be able to finance their housing through the free market, with their savings and assisted by a down-payment subsidy or a subsidised loan provided by the state (Baindur & Kamath, 2009).

Most countries opted for promoting housing markets and individual home ownership, privatising social housing programmes and deregulating housing finance markets (Rolnik, 2012). The global focus was also on developing housing finance mechanisms to enable households to take a mortgage (UN-ECE, 2005; The World Bank, 1988).

When privatisation did not result in a market for affordable housing, the World Bank modified its stance (The World Bank, 2000) and formulated new ways to mobilise private investment in affordable housing and urban services. Decentralisation and accountability through market mechanisms represented "a recasting of the debate by the IFIs from the promotion of outright privatisation of urban services to the commercialisation of urban service delivery", while ensuring accountability through the deployment of client power (Baindur & Kamath, 2009). Commercialisation of urban services was defined as making changes in institutional and financial management that facilitated the shift from public financing to private financing, such as user fees, municipal bonds, and forms of debt; and from public provision to private design, operations, and delivery of services through outsourcing, contracting, and public–private partnerships.

Further research (De Soto, 2000; Payne, 2001b) argued that the restrictive regulatory frameworks in most developing countries were responsible for widespread informality. The logical step in improving housing conditions in these countries was to remove such constraints on the housing process. The World Bank's subsequent World Development Reports in 2002 and 2004 argued for easing the regulations to make institutions work for the poor. The Bank has also been publishing an annual *Ease of Doing Business Report* to record the progress achieved by each country in simplifying regulations in various sectors.

The World Bank thus combined the lowering of regulatory barriers and addressing constraints to the availability of land and credit, with the commercialisation of urban services through user fees, municipal bonds, and forms of debt, and by promoting public–private partnerships.

What has India done so far to resolve the issue?

Urban housing policy and practice in India and Chhattisgarh

The Government of India (GoI) has, over the years, embarked on a variety of innovative housing programmes and policies, especially for lower-income households in urban areas. However, the coverage of these programmes and schemes is marginal when compared to the overall housing requirements of the urban population (Sivam & Karuppannan, 2002; Willis & Tipple, 1991). As mentioned earlier, in Chhattisgarh and Kolkata, the government-constructed affordable housing does not even meet 10% of the demand.

Indian housing policy at the national level gives a general direction to state housing policies and programmes. It also guides the central government's resource allocation to the state governments. This is done through various centrally sponsored schemes, and by setting the agenda for national financial institutions that are funded by the Government. The state governments receive the majority of their funding from the centre; however, the centre grants funds only for programmes that are aligned with the national policy. For this reason, states align their housing policies with the national policy, but they may and often do have their own state-sponsored schemes. While the central funding is routed through the concerned state department, the implementation and administration of many national schemes lie to a large extent with urban local bodies (ULBs) which are part of the local self-government structure.

The issue of low-end urban housing at the national level in India is the concern primarily of the Ministry of Housing and Urban Poverty Alleviation (MoHUPA). MoHUPA designs housing schemes for the poor as part of its larger mandate for urban poverty alleviation and issues scheme-related guidelines to all states. Accordingly, the ULBs prepare site-specific Project Reports and, through the state government, submit it to MoHUPA for sanction.

Such schemes are called central-aided schemes, and they have three components of funding: central grant (80%); state grant (10%); and the ULB's share (10%). The ULB may, if it considers it feasible, demand and receive a contribution from the beneficiary, but they never do.

Once the Project Report is sanctioned by MoHUPA, the central grant comes to the state government. The state government adds its share and transfers the fund to the ULB, which adds its own share to the fund. The entire funds are managed and spent by the ULB.

The actual construction of dwelling units in terms of the sanctioned Project Report is always done by private sector contractors. The selection of these private contractors is through a tender process. It can be done directly by the ULB, or the ULB may engage the services of other state agencies such as the Housing Board. When such an agency is involved, the agency charges the ULB a 'supervision charge' that can range from 2% to 10%. This ultimately gets added to the cost of the dwelling unit.

The Ministry of Urban Development (MoUD) administers the infrastructure development and slum upgrading programmes. Both ministries – MoHUPA and MoUD – have their own state-level implementation agencies, the State Urban Development Authority and the Urban Development Department.

India liberalised its economy in 1991, which included opening up to international trade and investment, deregulation, privatisation, tax reforms, and inflation-controlling measures (Topalova, 2005; Banga & Das, 2012). Based on the recommendations of the IFIs, the GoI came up with the National Housing & Habitat Policy, 1998. The objectives of this policy were clear; it sought to establish the market as the dominant mode of housing provision, at least in urban areas (MoHUPA, GoI, 1988; NHB, 1999). Although the GoI could itself adopt neo-liberal policies, it could not dictate such policies at the state level. The GoI could only recommend the state governments to privatise their housing markets.

Privatisation of the housing market in Chhattisgarh

The government of Chhattisgarh has adopted several recommendations over the years. Starting in 2000, GoCG abolished the housing board and privatised the housing sector to encourage a free market. While those efforts did lead to growth in the housing market, it was confined to the upper-income segments and did not result in a market for affordable housing. In 2004, the Chhattisgarh government restored the public provision of affordable housing, and the state housing board was re-created to "fill a vacuum" (CGHB, 2007), a term which aptly summarises the housing provision for the poor from 2002–2004, the trial period for the privatisation of the housing market.

Raipur is also one of 65 pilot cities in India that are implementing the GoI's Jawaharlal Nehru National Urban Renewal Mission (NURM) programme, a massive city modernisation scheme launched in 2005 with a total investment of over 20 billion USD over seven years. The urban housing component of the NURM is a project called Affordable Housing in Partnership. Private builders were not interested in this scheme, and even the response from the public housing authorities was unenthusiastic, with only two states opting to implement it. Chhattisgarh was one of these, and 3740 dwelling units were sanctioned under the scheme in Raipur and built by the housing board. The state continues to work on the reforms agenda prescribed under the NURM.

Raipur, therefore, offers an opportunity to identify and understand the institutional constraints in a state which claims to have a private-sector-friendly Housing Policy.

Being aware of the limited resources for the public provision of housing, the State Housing Policy of 2004 emphasised the need for private sector participation in affordable housing by "strengthening the role of government as a facilitator" and "creating an enabling environment by undertaking legal and regulatory reforms" (Housing Policy of Chhattisgarh, 2004). The Chhattisgarh government undertook several of the mandated legal and regulatory reforms, such as revision of the Rent Control and Land Acquisition acts, mandatory reservation of 15% land and 10% housing for poorer households in every housing project, and creation of a shelter fund to pay for either infrastructure development or land. The state housing board also served as a guarantor to ensure credit supply to poorer households which were buying dwellings in their projects. To address issues of credit and housing finance, the National Housing Bank and the Housing and Urban Development Corporation (HUDCO) were set up at the national level. Chhattisgarh has not revised its housing policy since 2004.

The World Bank's housing market enabling strategy and measures taken by the Indian and the Chhattisgarh governments

The World Bank's strategy for enabling housing markets includes both demand-side and institutional interventions. On the demand side, the strategy recommends that property rights should be developed through systems of private, tradable, and enforceable rights. Land should be registered, and insecure tenure should be regularised, and whenever possible these programmes should go hand in hand with infrastructure improvement in slum and squatter settlements, and they should recover their costs. Governments should seek to transfer publicly owned housing to residents and should involve the private sector in the administration and maintenance of public housing.

There is already a system of private, tradable, and enforceable property rights in India, but there is a need for the land mapping systems to be improved; this is being addressed by the state government, and land tenure and ownership rights that arise from slum upgrading programmes and infrastructure improvements in slum and squatter settlements are "regularised" every 10 years, while government-built housing is transferred directly to homeowners.

The World Bank recommends that the development of mortgage lending must go hand in hand with overall financial sector development. Financial policies should permit institutions to borrow and lend at positive real interest rates and on equal terms with other institutions. Competition should be encouraged to improve efficiency. Mortgage instrument designs should permit the interests of both borrowers and lenders to be realised through appropriate terms, especially indexing provisions, and collateral should be provided by well-designed and enforced systems of titling and foreclosure. Governments should encourage innovative institutional arrangements for promoting greater access to housing finance by the poor, such as mutual guarantees and flexible payment schedules, and lending for the provision of rental housing – which houses the majority of the poor in many developing-country cities – should be facilitated.

The Indian government established the National Housing Bank in 1988 to foster Housing Finance Corporations (HFCs), and they also set up various other initiatives, such as the Rajiv Rinn Yojna or India Mortgage Guarantee Corporation Pvt. Ltd., for developing low-income housing mortgage finance. The total housing credit outstanding in India in 2013 was some Rs. 76 billion, or about 1 billion USD. The Indian housing to GDP ratio is around 9%, which indicates the quality of lending to the sector, though it is lower than many other developed and developing countries. The loans of up to Rs. 500,000, or 6700 USD, to the poorest people made up under a quarter of this total because most such people lacked the necessary proofs of identity and address. In 2009, the government initiated a system to provide a unique identity to every Indian citizen but it takes time to cover the whole population.

The World Bank is generally against long-term subsidies and recommends that governments should see them as either transitional or a last resort. They should first try other methods for improving access to housing, such as regularizing insecure tenure, improving access to market-rate housing finance, removing barriers to the construction of rental housing, or improving housing supply markets to reduce prices. If subsidies are necessary, they must be well targeted, based on household numbers rather than dwelling units, measurable, and transparent, and should avoid distorting housing markets. Subsidies such as rent control are inequitable; they distort markets and reduce housing supply and should be avoided. One-time capital grants and housing allowances are usually more appropriate.

India has responded to these recommendations in various ways. The Rajiv Awas Yojana programme was introduced in 2011 with the stated objective of making India slum free. A quarter of the homes that are to be provided to slum dwellers are intended to be for rent, and in 2013 a task force on ways to spur the growth of rental housing in India mandated that rent controls should be scrapped, although subsidised housing schemes were continued.

The Twelfth Five-Year Plan document of 2011 stated that subsidies should be the last resort. It acknowledges that affordable housing is a particularly critical concern for India and states that India should meet the challenge through policies and incentives that will bridge the gap between price and affordability. Two other recent reports also acknowledged that it would be unrealistic to assume that slum dwellers would be able to afford "access to the burgeoning supply in the market" and that poorer people "cannot afford housing at current prices, and capital and/or interest subsidies are required" (MoHUPA, GoI, 2012a).

On the supply side, the World Bank recommended that continued attention should be given to improving residential infrastructure in slum and squatter settlements and extending it to new areas. The agencies responsible for residential infrastructure such as roads, drainage, water, sewerage, and electricity should focus less on narrow physical objectives and more on opening up urban land for residential development. This involves greater coordination in planning and possibly joint acquisition of rights of way, joint financing, and joint cost recovery. Infrastructure agencies should devote more attention to local demand, and existing communities should be encouraged to participate in planning and building infrastructure projects, to ensure accountability and smooth implementation. Cost recovery mechanisms need to be improved and when possible, infrastructure provision and maintenance should be privatised.

The Government of India and the State Government of Chhattisgarh have addressed these issues in various ways. The NURM slum upgrading programmes focus on improving residential infrastructure in slum and squatter settlements, and in Chhattisgarh, the state has pioneered the development of zoning regulations, such as reserving 25% of land and housing for poorer people. This measure was taken up by the Government of India and is part of the national guidelines for affordable housing. It was not clear, however, according to the estimates of the McKinsey Global Institute (2010), whether sufficient resources would be made available for this, as the annual outlay for infrastructure would have had to be increased from 0.5% of GDP to 2%.

It is also recommended that governments should seek to create greater competition in the building industry by eliminating regulatory barriers to entry, breaking up monopolies, facilitating equal access of small firms to markets and inputs, removing constraints to the development and use of local building materials and construction methods, and reducing trade barriers that apply to housing inputs.

The World Bank suggested that there should be a balance between the costs and benefits of regulations that influence urban land and housing markets, especially land use and building. The regulations should benefit rather than penalise the poor. Urban regulations should be audited in order to accomplish this, to establish their impacts on housing demand, supply, and prices and to set priorities for regulatory reform. New, affordable standards that do not compromise environmental, health, and safety concerns should be considered, and financial regulations must facilitate rather than hinder mortgage lending.

The government is the largest provider of affordable housing in Chhattisgarh; there is no restriction against private firms, but the rules do not allow the development of a competitive market for this type of housing. The Indian Central Building Research Institute was set up to work on low-cost construction techniques including building materials, construction technology, fire engineering, and disaster mitigation construction, and other organisations work in this field, but there has been little practical application of the results of their work.

Finally, it was suggested by the World Bank that governments at all levels should promote the development of appropriate institutions which would take up these policies. While the private sector should generally implement the policies, governments at state and local levels should monitor and, when necessary, amend regulations both as applying to housing standards and the provision of finance and any subsidies.

The Government of India established a number of programmes and institutions in order to achieve these objectives. These included the 'Strengthening Urban Management Programme' in collaboration with USAID and the World Bank and the City Managers Association of India, together with the National Housing Bank.

In spite of various efforts in the 1990s to promote a market in affordable housing, there was little or no private investment in the field, so the public authorities themselves took on the role of state enterprises, quite contrary to the principles of the enabling approach that the World Bank promoted.

In Chhattisgarh, while the state agencies mirror the practices of and compete with speculative developers in the market for higher-priced housing, employing land banking, aggressive marketing campaigns, and competitive building practices, they still retain the practice of allotment for subsidised housing for poorer people. A committee that is usually headed by the District Collector, the senior representative of government in each district, selects the households which will be allowed to buy low-cost dwellings built by the government agencies. These agencies build a certain number of dwellings every year for the urban poor. They are subsidised by varying amounts under different housing schemes. The number of dwellings falls far short of the actual demand, and therefore the applications are screened based on certain criteria. Even then, the number of eligible candidates usually exceeds by three or four or even ten times the number of dwellings available. The committee conducts a lottery, and those selected are allowed to buy the dwellings.

Another point of difference between private developers and the state enterprises is that public housing operates on the principles of cross-subsidy. Low-cost housing is subsidised and middle-income units are sold with little or no profit, whereas the prices of high-income houses and apartments are set at market levels. This is done to subsidise the cost of low-income housing with the profit from higher-priced homes.

However, this gives rise to two major concerns. First, even if the government builds more units for the urban poor than for the rich, in terms of total resources, far more is needed to satisfy wealthier customers' demands. Sengupta and Tipple (2007) and Sivam and Karuppannan (2002) quote Ansari (1989): 85% of the expenditure in India by the Housing Board benefits upper- and middle-income households, whereas only 15% is spent on housing for the urban poor. It is difficult to get the approximate amount spent on each income category sector, as every housing development has all kinds of units, and the dearth of information and lack of transparency in government operations that are typical in South Asia make it very difficult to make such calculations.

Another criticism is that the public authorities generate so few dwellings in comparison to demand that it makes no significant impact on the availability of low-income housing.

Commercialisation of infrastructure and urban services

Along with the privatisation of housing, the Eighth Five-Year Plan (1992–1997) continued its focus on recovering the costs incurred by local governments in providing urban infrastructure services. The 74th Constitutional Amendment Act in 1992 introduced wide-ranging urban sector reforms to strengthen municipal governance. In 1994, an Expert Group on Commercialization of Infrastructure projects was set up, which published the India Infrastructure Report in 1996. This report recommended moving away from state subsidies and towards private sector participation in urban infrastructure by accessing capital markets through municipal bonds. The Ministry of Urban Development launched several urban development schemes, including the Mega Cities Loan, the Urban Reforms Incentive Fund, and the City Challenge Fund. For the first time, budgetary allocations were linked to the implementation of specific policy reforms by the state governments (Baindur & Kamath, 2009).

This idea of raising funds from the market was reinforced during the Ninth Five-Year Plan (1997–2002), with a substantial reduction in budgetary allocations for infrastructure development. In 2004, it was recommended that state or local governments should be able to take future loans directly and that national guarantees should be phased out (Twelfth Finance Commission, 2004). "Cities were being starved of central government funding and compelled to undertake development projects through borrowings from the market, generating user fees and/or loans from IFIs." (Baindur & Kamath, 2009)

This strategy was accompanied by several assistance programmes from the World Bank and the Asian Development Bank, such as opening municipal funds to offer financial support to cities or states which did not have sovereign guarantees for infrastructure development, technical guidance, and grants to cities and states for financial reforms. The United States Government aid programme, through its three-phase Financial Institutions Reform and Expansion Debt Project (1994–2008), helped develop models for market financing for local government projects (ibid.).

One instrument for raising funds was the Pooled Municipal Debt Obligation (The Economic Times, 2006); smaller municipalities were grouped together to form one large unit, so as to increase their creditworthiness. Also, in 1999, GoI declared tax-free status to municipal bonds to boost the municipal bond market (Satyanarayana, 2001). However, the municipal bonds market "has been effectively dead", reportedly because the larger and better-rated municipalities have sufficient funds and are reluctant to turn to the debt markets, while smaller municipalities are not creditworthy. In addition, investors are reluctant because they have concerns about the ability of municipalities to increase revenues and fund themselves in the face of regular political interference (Dalal, 2014). In many cases (Aggarwal, 2008; Down to Earth, 2008) the municipalities increased the fees, promising better services, but could not collect the entire amount due to political interference. Any money recovered went largely towards repaying the investors and the lenders (Baindur & Kamath, 2009). This meant that the paying customers were left without adequate services, leading to even worse collections in the following period.

Being able to raise municipal funds did not resolve the constraint of lack of infrastructure. Most municipalities were unable to utilise the funds; some projects looked for funds too early, there were bureaucratic delays, and the local authorities had limited implementation capacity or were unable to submit the necessary financial reports and utilisation certificates (Accountability Initiative, 2014; Thakur, 2009), and had to pay penalties to the lending agencies. From 2004–2009, the government paid close to Rs. 7 billion (93 million USD) in penalties to international financial institutions for non-utilisation of sanctioned loans. An estimate of such expenditure since 1991 suggests that the total figure is over 250 million USD. The Indian Finance Ministry reported that until 2008, there were 231 externally aided projects, of which over 40% were paying such charges (Thakur, 2009).

Public–Private Partnerships (PPPs)

The commercialisation of urban services in India, including housing, was formally launched in 2005 through the Jawaharlal Nehru National Urban Renewal Mission (from now on referred to as the NURM) for a seven-year period up to March 2012, which was later extended to 31 March 2014. The aim was to encourage cities to initiate steps for bringing phased improvements in their civic service levels and to set up public–private partnerships as a means for financing and delivering infrastructure.

The *Affordable Housing in Partnership* scheme was introduced in 2009 in 65 pilot cities, including Raipur, with the aim of "operationalising the strategy envisaged in the National Urban Housing & Habitat Policy, 2007" (MoHUPA, 2009). The cities chosen were those where "shortages of land for housing are driving unplanned growth and rising home prices and rentals to unsustainable levels". In 2006, the Asian Development Bank provided 2 million USD in technical assistance to the Government of India to set up partnership cells in the pilot cities. These were meant to develop the capacity to prepare, evaluate, and appraise partnerships in infrastructure, and to improve monitoring of the progress of the partnerships (ADB, 2006 updated 21 October 2013).

The selection criteria for the housing projects were defined in terms of a certain number of houses being reserved for the urban poor. The sale price of these dwellings had an upper ceiling which was to be set by the local government. A total budget of Rs. 5000 crores (approximately 650 million USD) was earmarked for the scheme. It encouraged a "market-based approach" by attracting private developers to build on their land, by granting zoning incentives such as land use conversion, and increased density measures for the construction of affordable housing to be allotted by the state government.

The states were encouraged to develop their own rules and regulations for improving the provision of land and innovative partnerships for affordable housing. However, in order to access the previously mentioned incentives and government funding, the projects had to be in collaboration with the government. Also, the builders would have to follow the requirements of the scheme, such as the system for the allotment of houses and house price determination by the government. The scheme could also be undertaken by a public housing authority without private sector participation. In practice, private builders were not interested in the scheme, which received a lukewarm response even from the public housing authorities, with only two states opting to join it. Chhattisgarh was one of the two states, with 3740 dwelling units being sanctioned under the scheme in Raipur.

This scheme was revised in September 2013 (MoHUPA, 2013). While the conditions for private sector participation in the scheme remained the same, the minimum floor space and income limits of urban poor were revised.

Other amendments included an effort to bring "all existing slums, notified or non-notified within the formal system and enabling them to avail the basic amenities that are available for the rest of the city". The operational definition for a slum is, "any compact settlement with a collection of poorly built tenements, mostly of temporary nature, crowded together, usually with inadequate sanitary and drinking water facilities in unhygienic conditions". However, only some of these slums are part of the notification that is circulated by municipalities, corporations, local bodies, or development authorities, and these are termed 'notified' slums.

This revision aimed to encourage the creation of more rental housing for the growing population who wished to rent, as became necessary when the 2011 census estimated that nearly 27.5% of the urban population was living in rented accommodation. A maximum time limit of 60 days was set for project approvals, and in order to ensure that as many projects were taken up as possible, it was decided that projects could be undertaken by government bodies or through public–private partnerships, or by private builders whereby the state offers incentives or facilities such as Transfer of Development Rights (TDR), increased density measures, or other concessions.

These conditions are in line with the World Bank's revised policy rec-ommendation of building partnerships as an initial step towards enabling markets. In spite of these regulatory reforms, and their attempts to address issues of land or credit, the government has not been successful in either enabling a market or securing private investment for affordable housing through these partnerships.

Why did the public–private partnership and commercialisation strategy fail?

The public–private partnerships that came up were usually managed by large transnational companies, which often had local offices. There were many protests against the high fees to international consultants, as it was questionable whether they could actually strengthen capacities within local governments (Baindur & Kamath, 2009).

Mukhopadhyay (2008) argues that the public–private partnership arrangements engender corruption. They operate in a generally corrupt environment with weak regulations, and the administration is not gener-ally capable of overseeing performance. Hence, private contractors can use poorer material than is mandated and can share the savings with supervisors and their superiors. He further argues that the focus is on using such partner-ships for the construction of infrastructure in order to generate commercial revenue from user fees, rather than for improving services or accountabil-ity. Infrastructure should be financed by taxes and should not be used for raising government revenue. The NURM also introduced a new system for property tax assessment, called the Capital Value System, to improve the ability of cities to generate revenues. This system introduces valuation based on market values of land as opposed to rental values, as are used in the prevailing Annual Rateable Value system of property taxation. The ratio-nale was that this would increase property taxes, especially in areas where land values are high. However, the generated revenues had to first be used to secure loans taken from IFIs. Paybacks were based on a projected 251% increase in monthly water and sewerage charges (in real terms) between 1996 and 2005 and a projected 123% rise in property tax collections from 2000 to 2004. When it came time to pay, the local councilors and engineers could only realise a small increase in property tax collections and tariffs, due both to political and affordability considerations. This benefitted the IFIs rather than strengthening the ability of urban local bodies to provide better services to their citizens (Baindur & Kamath, 2009).

The NURM's public–private approach gave greater agency to private cor-porations than to elected bodies, which ran a risk of subverting democratic institutions by keeping the local bodies out of implementation. This was done to avoid constant interference by local politicians in the implementa-tion of government schemes. In practice, however, it meant that there was no direct link between the local institutions and the contractors who were hired to do the work.

However, the local institutions had to pay the contractors with money they had borrowed directly from the international institutions and bear the exchange and interest rate risks of foreign loans. The local elected representatives were not consulted on decisions regarding tenders, selection of consultants, or performance benchmarks. Contractors were appointed and monitored through a parastatal body managed by government bureaucrats, not by elected officials.

As a result, the local institutions could not be held accountable – as the monitoring was done by parastatals, where frequent staff changes because of regular transfers made it difficult to follow up on the work of the contractors and external consultants. Second, without any regular services or regular fees, many local institutions became seriously overindebted (Jamwal, 2006; CASUMM, 2008).

In addition, the projects were all large, because it was assumed that private investors were typically interested in large projects with higher returns. The ULBs' capacity to absorb and manage large funds was never considered, and projects were prioritised not by social considerations but on the basis of their profitability. Private entities claimed that the projects lacked sufficient financial incentives and a clear implementation framework. These issues, as well as the problems of dealing with resistance from land owners when acquiring the large tracts of land required to undertake large infrastructure projects, made the proposition unattractive for private developers (Baindur & Kamath, 2009).

How can affordable housing be effectively promoted?

The Enabling Markets Strategy has faced criticisms on multiple grounds – that the speculative private market will not cater to the poor and that the most vulnerable groups will be adversely affected (Baken, 2003; Baken & van der Linden, 1992; Jones, 1996), or that the strategy would lead to overconcentration on private markets at the expense of other modes of housing provision and would exclude alternatives from serious policy consideration (Keivani & Werna, 2001).

Most people believe that it is very difficult to promote an affordable housing market because it is not commercially feasible – "for very obvious reasons, such as affordability, perceived risk and profit" (Giddings, 2007).

We have presented a number of attempts to enable such a market along with the various challenges, and it is clear that it is very difficult; why then do we continue to favour it? It is because we believe that the failure has been in the strategy, not the theory.

To begin with, we accept that the policy of enabling markets in affordable housing cannot effectively serve the housing needs of all the urban poor, but it might still be able to serve a section of the slum population. Those who believe that the market enabling strategy overemphasises the private market at the expense of other modes of provision are correct if we consider the housing needs of the "poor" as a whole. However, our study attempts to disaggregate the 'poor' and to focus on those who are poor but who may nevertheless be able and willing to pay for their own housing.

The market enabling policy and the discussion around it essentially pose the debate as being between two opposing poles: market-enabling on the one hand, with a minimal regulative state; and public provision on the other. We, however, believe that it may be more fruitful to see the market enabling policy as one part of a pluralist perspective that allows extensive regulation and direct public provision to complement the market process, while at the same time supporting market development (Cao & Keivani, 2013).

This approach calls for a serious examination of the standard criticism of enabling markets, namely that the policy underestimates major market and institutional failures in developing countries. The mixed results of the enabling strategy in these countries demonstrates the need to study why a market for affordable housing did not emerge in, for example, Raipur. Some authorities believe that the state should play a more complex, sophisticated role to support well-functioning property markets:

> Paradoxically, enabling involves not only decentralisation but also some form of centralisation; not only privatisation but also new kinds of public investment; not only de-regulation but also enforcement of new regulations; and not only demand driven development but also supply driven initiatives.
>
> (Mukhija, 2001)

This statement deserves to be examined.

Designing markets, in this sense, requires not only overcoming the barriers and addressing the constraints but also introducing a detailed set of rules and regulations that are contextualised to a given environment. The focus is on studying the working and requirements of particular markets well enough to "fix them when they're broken or to build markets from scratch when they're missing" (Roth, 2007).

Markets are no longer simply viewed as the coming together of supply and demand but are understood as being situated in a larger social context. The emphasis is on understanding the constitutive elements that make each market special:

> For example, supply and demand drive both stock markets and labour markets, but someone who wants to buy or sell shares in

a company goes through a very different procedure from that followed by a job seeker or an employer. Moreover, labour markets work differently from one another; doctors are not hired the way lawyers, professional baseball players, or new MBAs are.

(ibid.)

Markets are as much a product of political processes as economic entities. Economic theory supplies terms and frameworks for formulating and justifying market rules, while property rights, rules of exchange, unwritten norms, and a cultural context are all objects of political contention. All these are, at any given point in time, influenced not just by interested market actors who are selling or seeking to buy but also by legislators who codify market rules as law, by regulatory authorities, and even by the cultural context that establishes limits on admissible strategies and claims (Breslau, 2013). This implies that the process of market design, which might seem simple in theory, may actually lead to uncertain results due to the reality of sociopolitical and cultural complexities.

Conclusion

This discussion of the evolution of Indian housing policy allows us to explore the possibility of creating the conditions for a formal market in affordable housing, as a way of reducing the enormous shortage of housing for the urban poor. This proposed policy, in the context of discussions on housing policy in developing countries in general, and in India and Chhattisgarh in particular, would be an 'enabling policy' which enables the urban poor to have access to affordable housing. It will learn from past experiences with enabling policies, especially the importance of the government as a regulatory authority. By examining formal and informal constraints, and by restructuring the institutions, can the government come up with culturally and financially realistic standards of adequate shelter options, involving various tenures and incremental development options?

3

MAKING MARKETS WORK
FOR THE POOR

Is constructing a market for the poor economically feasible?

The first point that arises when exploring market options is whether or not the urban poor can afford to pay for their own housing. There have been many studies[1] on the ability of urban poor people in India to afford decent housing. However, before the Technical Committee on Slum Statistics published its report in 2010, there was no agreement on the number of slums and the slum population. It is therefore difficult to analyse the existing situation comprehensively. These studies have used their own definitions and followed different criteria and objectives, but there is one common conclusion – that the 'urban poor' is a broad category consisting of various sections with varying capacity to afford housing, and that at least a section of the urban poor are capable of and "generally willing to pay for services, provided they receive the kinds of services that they need and regard [the exchange] as good value for money".[2]

The stipulated measures in the "Affordable Housing in Partnership" scheme is a minimum floor area of 300 square feet and a maximum of 1200 square feet. Houses built in Chhattisgarh since 2012 conform to this range. The price of 500-square-foot houses built under Deendayal Awas Yojana[3] (2007–2008) was between Rs. 2.5–3.00 lacs (3300–4000 USD), depending upon location and other factors. The price of the housing is determined based on the actual cost of the house and the subsidies available. The cost of the house is determined by the lowest bid on that particular housing scheme project. The construction bid is open to private developers. The price of a dwelling for the very poor under one of the government schemes (New Atal Awas Yojana)[4] was fixed at Rs. 1.10 lacs (1500 USD), although the actual cost (2007–2008) was around Rs. 1.25 lacs (1600 USD). Similarly, the price of a flat under another government (JNNURM BSUP) housing scheme is expected to be between Rs. 1.75–2.00 lacs (2400–2700 USD). In all cases, the cost includes the infrastructure cost (drains and roads). The figures we quote in the paragraphs that follow show a similar classification based on

2014 and 2016 prices and income limits. These prices will not hold valid for 2020 or 2030. Therefore, such an exercise will have to be taken up regularly. The point here is that whatever the price, we need to examine if there are institutional (rather than economic) constraints that are stopping a market from coming together.

Formal housing in Chhattisgarh also needs to have five basic amenities – a toilet, drinking water, roads, drainage, and electricity – to get approval for the building plan. These dwellings were used as benchmarks for the affordability assessment during our fieldwork among the urban poor living in the slums of Raipur.

We were told by staff of the Chhattisgarh Government Housing Board that in 2008, the Board ruled that the poorest households, with an annual income of Rs. 60,000 (about 800 USD) or less, should be entitled to a home of 300 square feet at a cost of between Rs. 1.25 to 1.5 lacs, or about 1900 USD, including the cost of land and the necessary infrastructure. Less poor people, with incomes of up to double that amount, should have homes of between 425 and 500 square feet, costing between Rs. 2.2 and 3 lacs, or 3000–4000 USD.

In 2014, the Board changed these norms and included an element of subsidy. Very poor people with incomes up to Rs. 1 lac, or 1350 USD, per year were entitled to homes in central Raipur of between 300 and 400 square feet, costing between Rs. 2.65 and 3 lacs, or 3500 to 4000 USD; this was to include a state subsidy of Rs. 80,000, or about 1000 USD, or they might be allotted a similarly sized home without subsidy in Naya Raipur, outside the city centre, for between Rs. 2.65 and 3 lacs, or 3500 to 4000 USD. The less poor, earning up to Rs. 2 lacs (or 2700 USD) per year, could have homes of 425 to 500 square feet which would cost between Rs. 3.1 and 3.5 lacs, or 4000 to 4600 USD, including a reduced subsidy of Rs. 40,000, or 500 USD.

In 2016, advertisements for low-cost homes for households earning up to Rs. 1 lac, or 1350 USD, per year stated that the cost of a 500-square-foot home was Rs. 8.1 lacs, about 10,800 USD, with a down payment of Rs. 1.2 lacs, or 1600 USD.

In India, the norm is five times the annual income or 60 times the monthly income, as practiced by Nationalized Banks when making individual housing loans. In theory, these figures show that if a poor person could secure a mortgage of three times their annual income, which is the norm in India, they would be able to afford decent formal housing built as per government standards. This is a theoretical assumption, because the ability to pay monthly instalments and having enough savings to be able to afford the down payment varies with each family.

It is important to note here that there is no public low-income rental housing sector in India. New programmes under Rajiv Awas Yojana (RAY, JNNURM) were looking to encourage rental housing schemes. However, the new government that was elected in May 2014 announced its plans to make monthly housing mortgage cheaper than monthly rents, showing that it had preference for owner-occupied housing (NDTV, 2014).

This is in theory, so we decided to test it empirically. The hypothesis was put to test in a random sample of 211 households from 21 slums in the Raipur Municipal Corporation (RMC) area; we calculate that the findings can be reported with a 92% confidence level and a 6% margin of error. According to the 2011 census, the number of slum households in Raipur was 80,200. The recommended sample size, using the "Raosoft" calculator (see https:// surveysystem.com/sscalc.htm) to be able to make a generalisation for Raipur, is 384 households, with a 95% confidence level and a 5% margin of error. But surveying such a large sample would have resulted in not being able to cover all three phases of the fieldwork; hence, a smaller sample was used. The survey was conducted in the slums of Raipur. Raipur is divided into 8 zones and 70 wards. According to the most recent data (2009, projected) from the RMC, there are approximately 282 slum areas in Raipur, with a total population of about 500,000 people, or 65,000 households. Their approximate locations are shown with stars in the map shown in Figure 3.1.

We interviewed 211 households from 21 slums spread across 16 wards of the Raipur Municipal Corporation area. Table 3.1 lists the slums that we surveyed.

The slums differ in their geographical locations, and therefore in their access to various amenities. Though most slums have mixed groups, some slums are divided on the lines of people's occupations, such as the iron-smiths in Lohar Para, and/or by regional communities that are defined by where they migrated from – such as Odisha or Madhya Pradesh – or are local *Chattisgarhias*, as people from the same caste or location tend to reside together. To reduce the anomalous effects of such systematic differences, the data was collected from different slums rather than from 211 households from one slum or one ward.

How much can they afford to pay for their own housing?

In order to assess slum dwellers' ability to pay, two hypothetical houses were generated. The prices were estimated at Rs. 300,000 (approximately 4000 USD) for the 300-square-foot house, and Rs. 500,000 (approximately 7000 USD) for the 500-square-foot house. Based on this, the Equated Monthly Instalments (EMI) and initial deposit were calculated. The estimated price of the house was arrived at by adding inflation to the 2008 price fixed by GoCG. The government agencies usually work on a no-profit, no-loss basis, but they do charge a processing fee of 10%, and an additional 10% is charged by the private contractor who executes the bid for the government housing projects (see Chapter 2). The final prices for 2012 were approximated at Rs. 3 and 5 lacs for 300-square-foot and 500-square-foot dwellings, respectively.

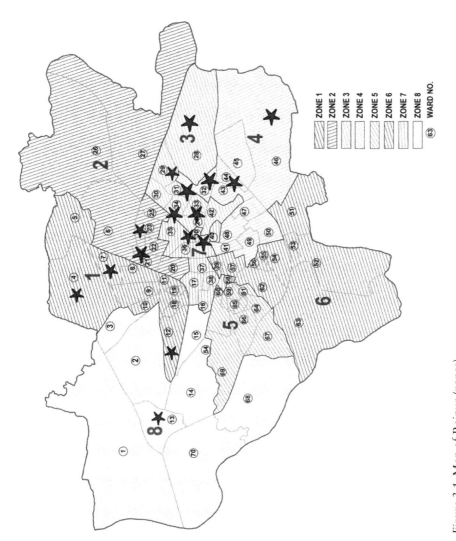

Figure 3.1 Map of Raipur (zones)

Source: Authors' construction, based on Raipur zonal maps

Table 3.1 List of slums surveyed

Zone no.	Ward no.	Locality	Ward
1	4	Gondwara	Yatiyatanlal Ward
8	13	Veer Shivaji Nagar	Bhagat Singh Ward
1	7	Srinagar	Veer Shivaji Ward
2	21	Jagrutee Nagar	Raman Mandir Ward
2	23	Kali Nagar, Fafadih	Rani Laxmi bai Ward
3	31	Gorkha Colony	Shanker Nagar Ward
3	34	Behra Colony, Pandri	Guru Goving Singh Ward
4	32	Meera Nagar	Veer Narayan Singh Ward
4	32	Bhola Nagar	Veer Narayan Singh Ward
3	29	Bajarang Chowk, Satnami Gali, Khamardih	Subhash Chandra Bose Ward
4	46	New Durga Nagar, Behind Ashoka Millenium	Rajendra Prasad Ward
3	28	Durga Nagar, Khamardih	Maharishi Valmiki Ward
3	28	Bhawna Nagar, Khamardih	Maharishi Valmiki Ward
4	44	Ravigram, Telibandha	Guru Ghasidas Ward
4	44	Railway Colony, Telibandha	Guru Ghasidas Ward
3	29	Shakti Nagar	Subhash Chandra Bose Ward
1	12	Krishna Nagar, Mahant Talab, Kota	Shahid Manmohan Singh Bakshi Ward
7	40	Mantralay Parisar	Babu Jagjeevan Lal Ward
3	33	Shanti Nagar	Lal Bahadur Shashtri Ward
3	30	Gandhi Nagar	Kalimata Ward
3	31	Shanker Nagar	Shanker Nagar Ward

Chapter 7 examines how these prices compare to market prices. These prices are comparable to the government dwellings, as we described earlier.

The two 'model houses' presented in the following section were used to assess the capacity to pay. Before asking the questions about the 'ability to buy', the calculations as detailed in the next paragraph for both houses were explained to each household. Any questions or clarifications were answered before proceeding with this part of the survey. The usual questions were: Where would these be located? Who is the developer? Is the government involved in some way? The households were reminded that these were hypothetical questions that would help in gauging the slum dwellers' capacity to pay. They were assured that there was no right or wrong answer and were encouraged to be honest in their answers in order to help the study to arrive at a fairly accurate approximation, and thus to be useful.

The current rate of interest (2019) for formal housing loans is 8%, but in 2012, it was higher – between 11% and 13% (NHB, 2012b). The initial deposit is usually fixed by the bank,[5] and it is between 15% and 20% of the loan amount. For this study, it was assumed to be 20%, because of the higher risk involved in lending to slum dwellers. Banks offer 15- to 20-year long-term loans; the duration of the loan term is chosen by the customer. The loan has to be repaid within the term specified, and if it is paid off early there is a small penalty. A 15-year repayment cycle was used for our calculations. With this data, the following figures were arrived at using a mortgage calculator (see www.icicibank.com/Personal-Banking/loans/home-loan/homeloan-emi-cal.html):

1) For the Rs. 300,000 dwelling at 12% and 15 years:

   – 20% deposit = Rs. 60,000
   – Actual loan amount = Rs. 300,000–60,000 = Rs. 240,000
   – So, as per the EMI calculations:
   – Loan = Rs. 240,000
   – Interest rate =12%
   – No. of years = 15
   The Equated Monthly Instalments (EMI) figure, in this case, is Rs. 2880, or about 40 USD

2) For the Rs. 500,000 dwelling at 12% and 15 years:

   – 20% deposit = Rs. 100,000
   – Actual loan amount = Rs. 500,000–100,000 = Rs. 400,000
   – So, as per the EMI calculations:
   – Loan = Rs. 400,000
   – Interest Rate =12%
   – No. of years = 15

   The Equated Monthly Instalments (EMI) figure, in this case, is Rs. 4800, or about 65 USD

The housing affordability was assessed using these figures. At current (2019) interest rates, this amount would have been much lower.

The two widely used definitions of measuring affordability are the ratio method and the residual method. The ratio method is expressed as a percentage of a person's income that is spent on rent, which is usually set at 30% of income and is normally applied to the whole population, nationally or locally. However, this method has been criticised on the grounds that a single ratio cannot account for regional variations in housing costs, nor does it distinguish between households with the same income levels but different household sizes. The residual method refers to the amount of cash a household is left with after accounting for its essential expenditure. The interpretation of this method depends on defining adequate standards and on the consistency of cost-of-living measures across areas and households (Freeman, Kiddle, & Whitehead, 2000).

Sensitivity Analysis: If the interest rate were higher (16% or 20%) to take into account the extra costs of relatively small loans, or the extra risk of lending to poorer households, the EMI would be as follows:

For the Rs. 300,000 house at 16% and 15 years – Rs. 3525
For the Rs. 300,000 house at 20% and 15 years – Rs. 4215
For the Rs. 500,000 house at 16% and 15 years – Rs. 5875
For the Rs. 500,000 house at 20% and 15 years – Rs. 7025

In this study, the affordability measure was based on the residual method, whereby the households themselves defined their adequate standards of non-housing needs and the associated expenditure. They were encouraged to discuss among themselves and decide whether or not they could afford the initial deposit and the monthly instalment for the housing, after accounting for their essential expenditure. This helped reduce the possible biases of households falsely reporting that they could afford to buy the dwelling in order to avoid embarrassment. It also helped to serve as a check against families who underreported their income. In such cases, the details of their expenditure would exceed their income levels, and they would then admit to an additional source of income that was initially not reported.

However, this measure of affordability does not include the cost of daily public services such as electricity and water charges, or maintenance costs connected to the units. The households were reminded that moving into such housing would mean incurring such additional charges. This affordability measure also does not include additional costs for transportation that they might have to incur in the case of moving to a location further from the city centre. Currently, not many of the slum dwellers use public transport. The women reported that their places of work were within 2 to 5 kilometres' distance from their homes, and the distances for men were between 5 and 8 kilometres. They usually covered this distance on foot or by cycle. Reliance on shared auto services in the city was reported only for personal entertainment, such as going to watch a movie or to go shopping. As mentioned earlier, living within 5–8 kilometres from a market centre and/or residential complex where they would find work was reported by 30% households as a prerequisite in their decision to buy new housing.

The term 'investment' rather than 'buying a family home' is used in discussing the findings, as during the fieldwork it was revealed that some households in the slums were considering buying a house to rent to others, at least temporarily. Every one of the surveyed families, including very poor and poor households, considered the investment to be 'value for money'. However, when they were asked if they would be willing to invest in the model home, 84% of the 94 very poor households we spoke to said that they would be willing, and 92% of the less poor households agreed. Those who said that they would not be willing had various reasons to be 'currently' not willing, such as an upcoming wedding in the family, they did not feel the need to buy a new home, or they had other priorities. The question about willingness to buy was asked before the question about ability to pay.

We had to make it clear that we were asking people whether they were able to buy such a home immediately in order to avoid the more casual, "we will think about it when such homes start getting built" answer. However, it also meant that many families had an upcoming priority that they needed to attend to, and therefore were "currently" not willing.

The households were informed about both housing options, as many poor families had, in answering the earlier questions, indicated that they would be satisfied with the smaller model house that was intended for the poorest people. They were then asked if they considered themselves financially able to buy one of the two homes. Sixty-five percent of the poorest people and 95% of the less poor said that they were able to buy one of the two model houses.

More detailed analysis, including an assessment of their expenditure patterns based on current subsidies, indicates that 102 out of the 170 households, or 60%, could afford to buy a house within their own category, meaning that a very poor household could buy a house for Rs. 300,000, and a less poor household could pay Rs. 500,000. Fifty-four of the lowest-income households could only afford a 300-square-foot home, while 16 of them reported that, while they could buy it at that time, in the case of an emergency – such as someone falling sick or meeting with an accident, or in the case of the state withdrawing its food subsidies – they would not be able to afford the EMI.

In effect, 74% of the surveyed population[6] indicated that they could afford to buy a house of one or the other design, and 18% were clear that they would not be able to afford such a home. The remaining 8% said that they might not be able to sustain repayments, as their capacity to pay was highly dependent on other factors. It is important to note that the survey excluded approximately 20% of the households who lived in the slums but said that their earnings were above the 'poor limit' set by the government.

In summary, three-quarters of the slum dwellers said that they were both willing and able to pay the full cost of a 'pukka' fully serviced house and its financing. This demonstrates the scale of the demand.

Are the suppliers interested?

Naturally, the next question was to seek the developers' opinions on whether it would be technically feasible to build such housing within the cost estimated. There were 77 developers listed as being members of the Confederation of Real Estate Developers Associations of India, Chhattisgarh Chapter (CREDAI-CG). CREDAI is the apex body for private real estate developers in India and represents over 6000 developers through 18 member associations or local chapters across the country. Thirty of these 77 developers, which are listed alphabetically in the chapter's membership list, were interviewed. Every alternate developer was approached for the interview until the target of 30 interviews was met. If a developer was unavailable, the next on the list was interviewed. None of the 77 developers refused an interview. One had met with an accident and was recovering; two were on family vacations, while three were away on business. These six developers were more than willing to give an interview provided it could be postponed, but because we were on a tight time schedule, the next developer on the list was interviewed.

Most of the interviews lasted about an hour, although some took only 45 minutes or up to 1.5 hours, and two took more than 2 hours. The interviews were mostly conducted in Hindi; these were later transcribed and then translated into English. The interviews were conducted either at the respondents' business or site offices. Most of the businesses were family owned, and in one interview, both father and son participated. The interviewees included 16 small developers, 6 mid-sized building firms, 4 large building firms, and 4 very large building firms, where the size of the firm was defined by the number of dwellings they had built the year before. Small developers were defined as those who had constructed 0–49 dwellings in the previous year; mid-sized firms had constructed 50–99 dwellings; large firms had constructed 100–199 dwellings; and very large firms had built 200–400 dwellings.

All of the developers interviewed built housing for middle- and high-income levels, as well as for the 'luxury segment' as it is commonly termed in Raipur. House prices ranged from Rs. 15–35 lacs (20,000 USD to 46,000 USD) for the middle-income range; up to Rs. 70 lacs, or 93,000 USD, for high incomes; and up to 4 crores or 40 million rupees, about 535,000 USD, for the 'luxury segment'.

There were a few[7] small developers who were also building what they called low-income houses – with houses ranging from Rs. 7.5–15 lacs.[8] The developers said that the type of housing was determined primarily by the location of the available land but also by the demand. Most private developers in Raipur are builders as well as developers. They buy land on the private market and develop housing and commercial complexes. A few[9] also undertake contract work for the government. None of the 30 developers whom we interviewed were building dwellings in the price range of between Rs. 3 lacs and Rs. 5 lacs, which we consider to be 'affordable' housing.

These developers are businesspeople operating in a speculative real estate and construction industry, and they would naturally like to participate in the potentially large market of poorer people (Interviewees 06B and -03B specifically stated this). More than 100 million people in India fall into the category of the urban poor, and it has been estimated that by 2030, more than 400 million Indians will be living in cities. In 2019, one in every six of India's urban households live in slums, and this number is expected to rise exponentially over the coming years.

One developer (Interviewee-12B) who was talking about one of his ongoing projects mentioned that it had taken him six years to develop a single housing project, as 'luxury segment' homes come with unique specifications tailored to the customer's needs and changing preferences. The low-end market was mass housing and in the opinion of all 30 developers, it was a different kind of business, where profits were driven by high volume and turnover. They felt, however, that it is not economically viable because of official interference.

How much would a dwelling for the 'very poor' cost?

The first part of the developers' interviews included asking them to estimate the cost of building a 300-square-foot low-cost house with the five basic amenities – that is, water, electricity, drainage, roads, and toilet – at market prices in Raipur. The developers estimated that some changes in official rules would allow them to construct dwellings for below Rs. 300,000; this confirmed that such a dwelling could be built at current levels of cost.

The average estimates from the 30 developers are presented in Table 3.2. The cost of land varies depending on where the land was situated – for example, the northeast of the city was considered expensive, as it was closer to the higher-income residential areas of the city and the airport, while the land in the southern lower-income area was considered to be worth only half as much. The cost of construction depends on the developer and the reputation he has in the market, where smaller firms quoted Rs. 800 per square foot and larger firms mentioned needing Rs. 1000 per square foot for quality construction. Larger firms generally looked for higher profit margins than smaller firms.

Table 3.2 Estimated cost of a 300 sq. ft. dwelling under present rules

Estimated cost of a 300 sq. ft. dwelling calculated at an average floor area ratio of 1.45	Average estimated cost	Percentage of total cost	Approximate cost in USD
Land	84,300	20%	$1100
Construction cost	233,300	56%	$3100
Development cost (roads, playground, garden) + utilities (electricity, water)	42,000	10%	$560
Profit + overheads	57,500	14%	$800
Registration + taxes	Very poor households in CG are exempt from paying for registration and taxes. Otherwise, the developers gave an estimate of 8% of the total cost for registration and taxes.		
Total[10]	417,100	100%	$5500

Table 3.3 Cost of a 300 sq. ft. dwelling under a different set of regulations

Cost components	Average estimated cost in Rs.	Percentage reduction of the individual components	Reduced estimates if institutions were to change	Rules to be changed
Land	84,300	65%	29,200	Increase the average floor area ratio from 1.25 to 3.
Construction cost	233,300	9%	212,700	Tax exemptions on materials
Development cost (roads, playground, garden) + utilities (electricity, water)	42,000	30%	29,200	Through VAT exemption, fees waiver
Profit + overheads	57,500	20%	45,900	Incentives such as TDR, or income tax exemption on
registration and taxes	Very poor households in Chhattisgarh are currently exempt from paying for registration and taxes.			
Total	**417,100**	**24%**	**317,000**	

The average cost of a 300-square-foot dwelling was Rs. 417,100, or about 5500 USD. In one of the earlier interviews (Interviewee-02B), which also happened to be one of the longest interviews, there was a detailed discussion on the possibility of reducing this cost. According to this interviewee's estimate, which varied slightly from the average of the 30 developers even with a conservative assessment, 24% to 27% of the cost could be eliminated under different rules, as shown in the last column of Table 3.3. This was an estimate that all 30 developers agreed was fairly accurate. These rule changes included increasing the floor area ratio or density index, some tax exemptions, and incentives such as the inclusion of Transfer of Development ment Rights (TDR). A TDR makes a certain amount of additional development land available in an alternate location, such as might be suitable for a higher-income property in lieu of either the area relinquished or housing built for the urban poor, so that the developer can use the extra space or sell it to another developer who needs the extra built-up area:

A TDR programme seeks to preserve landowners' asset value by moving the right to build a house from a location where development is prohibited (e.g., for environmental reasons) to a location where development is encouraged. In the place where development

48

is encouraged under TDR, zoning is changed to permit more units to be built. This generates the opportunity to earn more money from development than landowners would have received in the absence of the TDR programme.

(NJ AES)

If the estimated cost could be reduced by 24%, then the cost would be Rs. 317,000. A staff member of Nirman Vikas Anusandhan Sansthan (NIVAS), an NGO in Raipur that specialises in low-cost housing and has built low-cost homes in Raipur for 12 years, revealed that the cost of the housing can be reduced further:

> 50% of cost optimisation is because of good planning; we plan it in such a manner that the length of services is minimal . . . we keep the length of the brick work to a minimum. For the same space, the materials required are minimum.
>
> (Interviewee-9F)

> In today's prices, we will need at least Rs. 125,000. It would be including sanitary, internal electrification, internal development, painting, doors, windows . . . everything. Of course, the profit of the contractor has to be taken into account. The cost that I mentioned to you is the actual cost and does not include profit. We work on a no-profit, no-loss basis and only include our overheads. But if you want to have a profit of 10 to 12%, then you have to add that to this . . . say Rs. 140,000 would be the maximum.
>
> (Interviewee-9F)

If the Rs. 82,000 average cost of land in Raipur is added to the quoted figure of Rs. 140,000, the total comes to Rs. 222,000. The NGO representative mentioned that they had been awarded a contract to build 1000 houses in Panipat, a city in North India, for Rs. 222,000, the cost quoted, which was to be completed by November 2012. The previous analysis allows us to infer that it is feasible to build a 300-square-foot home, including the five basic amenities, for very poor households for the stipulated figure of Rs. 300,000 (4000 USD).

When they were asked if they would be willing to enter the affordable housing market, all 30 developers responded positively, but they added that it would only be possible if the [institutional] constraints they experienced were addressed.

If there is potential demand and potential supply, then why is the market not coming together?

The two most important conclusions thus far are 1) more than 70% of the surveyed population[11] indicated that they could afford to buy one of the two model houses specified in the survey; and 2) private developers can be an alternate source for supply of affordable housing. This supports the hypothesis that in Chhattisgarh, it would be profitable for private developers to supply housing for many poor urban people, with the existing levels of cost and incomes. If there is potential demand and potential supply, then why is the market not coming together?

We must ask whether the existing institutional arrangements prevent the emergence of a market for low-cost housing in Raipur. Before we discuss this issue any further, we need to understand what an institutional structure is; or more simply, what are institutions?

What are institutions?

Institutions are "the rules of the game: the humanly devised constraints that structure human interaction" (North, 1993b). They are the "systems of established and prevalent social rules that structure social interactions" (Hodgson, 2006). Institutions give effect to the values and goals of a society. A society needs institutions "to satisfy the functional needs of the community (Knight, 1992)", as they reduce uncertainty by establishing a stable (though not necessarily efficient)[12] structure to human exchange (North, 1990b).

Some institutions continue to exist even when they are not efficient because they can create stable expectations of the behaviour of others. By imposing form and consistency on human activities, institutions both constrain and enable behaviour (Hodgson, 2006). Individuals may conform out of fear of loss of reputation from disobedience, or potential dissenters may fear that their opposition is doomed to failure, and thus, inability to challenge the system becomes a self-fulfilling prophecy. These self-reinforcing mechanisms for the persistence of institutions can be called path-dependent processes (Bardhan, 1989).

Institutions can be both formal and informal. Formal institutions usually follow written rules and include organisations, such as the legislation governing the production, exchange, and consumption of a product such as housing. Informal institutions could be social norms like caste and class divisions that organise a particular society and determine the housing patterns. These are some examples of societal norms that have economic implications and influence economic choices, not necessarily in a 'rational' manner.

Formal institutions are easier to change than informal ones, as they involve mostly 'political will'. Informal institutions are "self-enforced, in the sense that no external authority is available to guarantee that social actors will follow them" (Knight, 1992). They are self-stabilised, decentralised, and hence deep rooted, and changing them may involve behavioural change. If and when the formal institutions are weak, such as those that have ambiguous rules, job descriptions, or terms of reference, informal institutions are sometimes needed to strengthen their position.

PROPERTY RIGHTS

Property rights are the rules governing the use of resources (Ensminger, 1996). 'Rights' are the product of the 'rules', and thus are not the same as the rules. Eggertsson (1990) categorises property rights[13] as follows, providing instances where two or all three of the categories can blend:

1   The rights to use an asset, including the rights to transform physically or even destroy an asset.
2   The rights to earn income from an asset and contract over the terms with other individuals
3   The rights to transfer permanently ownership rights over an asset, that is to sell or donate them to another party.

The value of the rights determines the value of what is exchanged (Demsetz, 1967); therefore, restriction on rights that shrink the set of permissible uses will lower the economic value of an asset (Eggertsson, 1990). The value of the rights also depend on the enforcement characteristics. Government must play an essential role in enforcing contracts. The cost of enforcing these rights is reduced when social norms coincide with the basic structure of the rights that the state seeks to uphold (ibid).

TRANSACTION COSTS

The term[14] was coined by Kenneth Arrow (1969) in 'The Organization of Economic Activity', and he used it to distinguish transaction costs (from production costs) as the cost of running the economic system. North (1990a) gives a different definition; he recognises production costs as 'the sum of transformation[15] and transaction costs', where transaction costs relate to "the capital involved in defining and enforcing property rights over the good (the right to use, to derive income from the use of, to exclude others, to exchange) known as the transaction function". For Williamson (1993), transaction costs are those costs associated with the governance of contractual relations. Though over the years there have been many definitions, there is no theoretical consensus on what constitutes transaction costs. Allen (2000), after an exhaustive literature review, narrows it down to two categories:

> *Transaction Costs #1: The costs of establishing and maintaining property rights* – the costs of policing and enforcing agreements, while implicitly recognizing the threat of appropriation or theft.
>
> *Transaction Costs #2: The cost resulting from the transfer of property rights* – costs in an exchange – because parties to exchange must find one another, communicate and share information. There may be a necessity to inspect and measure goods to be transferred, draw up contracts, consult with lawyers or other experts, and transfer title.

Compliance with a complex system of regulations in a bureaucratic setup with low levels of enforcement increases both kinds of transaction costs. This makes the system inaccessible and prohibitive to all but a few privileged groups (Berner, 2001). According to the school of thought, institutions that evolve to lower these costs are the key to the performance of economies (Bardhan, 1989).

Why do institutions matter for the affordable housing market?

Most countries have a housing problem in some form,[16] and they all, regardless of their orientation towards free markets or central planning, have adopted a variety of housing policies. The production, consumption, financing, distribution, and location of dwellings are controlled, regulated, and subsidised in complex ways. Compared to other economic commodities, housing is perhaps the most tightly regulated of all consumer goods (Hårsman & Quigley, 1991).

Even radical proponents of a minimalistic state concede that the market cannot by itself set all the rules of the game. It does not bring about the preconditions for its own functioning, such as rule of law, guarantee of private property, or contract enforcement. Another need for regulation arises because an informal consensus about what the rules of the game are, does not guarantee how they are interpreted in specific cases (Berner, 2000). Institutions structure behaviours and exchanges in markets; they therefore often serve as a constraint in such markets. However, in addition, they can stimulate actions by providing predictability. The next section will analyse how institutions constrain the provision of low-cost housing.

Institutions determining the resource allocation

Resources in a society can be distributed through various mechanisms. They can be political, bureaucratic, a market distribution, or a mix of these. For example: Needham and de Kam (2004) illustrate how Dutch housing associations choose to acquire land through the mechanism of mutual trust when there is a network in place which they can use, and to acquire through the market when that mechanism is not available.

Institutions are often created to serve the interests of those with the bargaining power to create new rules (North, 1993b). Therefore, in order to understand the process of resource allocation, it is important to understand the concept of *bargaining power*. Individuals in a society have different levels of skill and access to information and other resources, and this determines their unique position in society. However, every individual is dependent on others for operating within the society. In order to be in a credible bargaining position, the party must have something to offer that the other party wants;[17] bargaining power is, therefore, the exploitation of asymmetrical interdependence, leading to a mutually beneficial economic relationship (Wagner, 1988). The particular outcome of a bargain depends on the objective of the exchange. The general outcome of a bargain is that both parties involved are in a better position, however largely or slightly, than before the bargain.

Power is the essence of bargaining, the "pivotal construct for a general theory of bargaining" determined by the bargaining position (Bacharach & Lawler, 1981). One could be in a better bargaining position because of various vantage points like better information, better bargaining skills, or less need than the other party.

Examining the current mode of allocation in affordable housing allows us to investigate whether a market would allow a larger number of households to have access to decent housing. In India, affordable housing serves the client–patron relationship[18] and is conspicuous on the political agenda. Thangavel (1998) discusses the Dravida Munnettra Kazhagam, a leading political party in Tamil Nadu in the south India government, using housing as a political manoeuvre and giving free homes to a section of the population (in exchange for votes), which led to big expectations and high dependency that put an undue burden on later projects, as people were reluctant and unwilling to pay the instalments.

Joop deWit and Berner (2009) find brokerage and patronage so ubiquitous in India that they call it 'institutionalised mediation' – a function of a lack of resources or services, access problems to agencies and institutions, and finally, a lack of enforced impersonal rules for the allocation of resources.

> There is evidence indicating that the urban poor prefer to rely on vertical patronage . . . based on the experience that investing in collective action is problematic, time-consuming and fraught with free rider problems. In contrast, using an intermediary or broker is perceived to increase the chance of obtaining a service or gaining protection against a threat. This calculation is obviously valid in the case of private needs and services such as shelter, jobs, credit. But even in the case of 'public goods' and collective services (paved alleys, piped water, public toilets, street lights) the poor usually have more faith in contacting intermediaries and politicians than in organising rallies to voice their demands or collective projects to meet their needs themselves. The skepticism of the urban poor with regard to collective action is confirmed by the glaring mismatch between the supply and demand of services critical to them, which in many cities is exacerbated by new demands created by rural – urban migration. The system benefits the political and city elites in two ways: they are able to influence the poor with a view to

obtaining their votes, while the poor are constrained from organis-
ing as a group or movement as they focus on individualised and
fragmenting vertical strategies . . . the consequence is a 'Faustian
bargain', a discounting of the future in favour of . . . the present",
that contributes to the status quo.

(deWit & Berner, 2009, pp. 928–929)

Gangopadhyay and Nath (2001) agree, as they assess the performance
of local governments and find that group dominance and bargaining
"frustrates local expenditure efficiency" in urban India. North (1993a)
emphasises the political process as a critical factor in the performance of
economies, whereby individuals and organisations with high bargaining
power as a result of the institutional framework have a crucial stake in
perpetuating the system.

In the light of the previous discussion, one may ask whether a market
alternative, when compared to the existing political, bureaucratic, and
clientelist allocation mechanisms, would increase the provision of low-
cost housing. By market alternative, we mean a market that is facilitated
by the state, rather than the concept of 'free market'. Such a market
would facilitate individual autonomy in terms of having a choice to be
able to buy a dwelling if the person has the means to afford it. Currently, the ability of an urban poor household to buy a formal dwelling
depends on a lottery allotment; if the household wins, it is then allowed
to buy the house. The problems of market failure are well known and
emphasised by those who favour bureaucratic allocation of resources.
However, when interest group politics dominate political decisions, the
bureaucratic allocation can advance private rather than public concerns
(Libecap, 2008).

Can institutions constrain a housing market from coming together?

The first step in testing a market alternative would be to examine the
factors that are stopping a formal housing market from coming together.
We refer to constraints created by man-made rules as 'institutional constraints'. Such rules could be explicit, made by the state, or implicit, such
as those enforced by culture or societal norms. These may constrain the
market in varying degrees. However, the government may or may not be
able to address them depending on how they influence other sectors – such
as lowering taxes, which may stimulate the market but also reduces government revenue. The existing literature on institutional constraints on
housing markets focuses on transaction costs, property rights, credit and
mortgage, and land supply.

Establishing private property rights

Establishing private property rights with secure tenure and effective and efficient title systems is not easy. It requires careful and deliberate land planning, with suitable land titling and property registration systems managed by an effective administration capable of enforcing them. Each of these requirements poses a challenge in countries such as India. While secure property rights reduce the transaction cost, when such a large proportion of urban residents lives in informal settlements in India and other developing countries, establishing secure tenure can be a very expensive process.

These rights can be formal, and captured in constitutions, statutes, or regulations; or informal, as in accepted norms of behaviour. So long as people respect them, both formal and informal property rights can work effectively. However, Boudreaux (2005) cautions that there is a very real risk that reforms enacted in the name of property rights will fail if policy makers employ the rhetoric of property rights, such as giving away titles, but do not consider how property rights function in the real world.

High transaction cost

If the cost of a transaction is too high, such that the costs of the item itself plus transaction costs are higher than the price people are willing to pay for the commodity, a market cannot operate. In housing, slums and squatter settlements are a case in point. Quoting from United Nations Centre for Human Settlements (UNCHS) statistics, Berner (2000) states that in the large cities of the developing world, between 30% to 70% of the population live in irregular settlements, and nearly 85% of the new housing stock is produced extra-legally. Here we examine how high transaction costs affect the system.

Blaming "an outmoded system of legal property", De Soto (2000) found that grassroots property arrangements "openly contradict the official written law", which his research claims is because the "written law is not in harmony with the way their country actually works". His research in several low-income countries established that the obstacles to entering the legal property systems are so daunting and expensive that few could ever make their way through the red tape. "To obtain legal authorization to build a house on state-owned land [in Lima, Peru] took six years and eleven months – requiring 207 administrative steps in 52 government offices. To obtain a legal title for that land took 728 steps" (De Soto, 2000, p. 18).

According to a World Bank report (2009), property owners in India often resort to strategies such as evading registration or using long-term leases, transfers under court decrees, and cooperative housing, to avoid property tax. Because of such practices, approximately 90% of the total time spent on registering property in the Indian cities sampled in the study is spent in verifying that the property is free of dispute. The remaining 10% of the time would take 55 days of work and cost 10.6% of the property's value, involving five procedures to register the property into one's name. The report mentions "backlogged caseloads" and "lack of staff" as the main causes of delay. The costs do not include the time taken, which was separately calculated as the number of days, or include stamp duties, accounting on average for 70% of all the costs incurred; the cost of stamp duty varies from 12.5% of the property value in Kochi to as low as 3% in New Delhi. Registration, legal fees, and brokers' fees also have to be paid. Registering the land is only the first of several steps which have to be taken before the developer gets permission to build.

Mahadevia, Sharma, Joshi, and Shah (2009) highlight similar issues in the supply of land for government agencies in India, where in most cases, clearance for land acquisition is difficult to obtain because the land is under litigation. By the time the clearance certificate is available, the costs of construction would have increased, and the rates on which the tender was awarded would be outdated. Such instances of land having numerous apparent owners are not unique to India. De Soto (2000) reports (p. 94) that only 7% of the land on the Indonesian archipelago has a clear owner, and that this leads to a flourishing trade in both genuine and forged certificates.

The World Bank has rated countries on the ease of doing business in the country. The rating depends on the number of steps involved and the number days it takes to complete processes, such as starting a business, dealing with construction permits, registering property, getting credit, paying taxes, or enforcing contracts. In 2014, India was ranked 134th out of 189 countries, which indicates that the transaction costs are very high, particularly in relation to low incomes and the small scale of the actual assets being transferred. After corruption and bribery (which are not included in the report) are included, the system is simply not affordable by the urban poor.

Credit and mortgages

The majority of the urban poor need a mortgage to be able to buy a house, but the housing finance system in India[19] is effectively not available to poorer people. Efforts to make housing finance available to low-income groups through NGOs and other community-based organisations have not been very successful (NHB, 2006), largely because they are still restricted to those who have the documents that are necessary to establish their incomes, such as government employees.

Peer Smets (2002), in his article 'Indian Housing Finance Alliances and the Urban Poor', discusses the various options that urban poor people in India have to secure housing finance. These include the SPARC/NSDF/MM Alliance[20] housing finance model, Igel and Srinivas' (1996) model for delivery of credit to squatter settlements in Bangalore, and the Dharavi Scheme in Mumbai.

There are various other credit schemes for housing the urban poor out-side India, such as the Urban Community Development Office scheme in Thailand and the Community Mortgage Programme in the Philippines. All of these are based on the principles of microfinance,[21] where beneficiaries are encouraged to organise themselves into community associations. These associations can then apply to a government body for a loan, and their applications can be supported by an NGO, a local authority, or a national housing agency. These organisations need to provide a guarantee for the loan and take responsibility for ensuring that documents are in order and that repayments are punctual.

If savings groups are supported to learn from each other, there is a good chance that "networks develop, creating stronger, larger groupings of the urban poor with a greater capacity to negotiate with external agencies and develop a common fund" (Boonyabancha, 2001). However, microcredit is built on the principles of group dynamics, and is therefore often not very sustainable due to 'natural' tensions between group members, which can affect any group (Bowden, 1990). The strength of community groups is also negatively affected by other factors, such as the high turnover of field work-ers from the facilitating NGOs, excessive assistance that creates dependence, the difficulty of fostering group cohesion and sustainability, the significant role of charismatic leaders, and problems in generating self-help decision-making capabilities. These problems are not uncommon in small groups that manage low-value, short-term loans but are all the more significant when larger, longer-term credit such as housing finance is involved. Another problem is that debts may be written off by politicians as a favour, which is a common practice in India.[22] Borrowers may anticipate such loan waivers and thus not repay their loans.

Land for low-income housing

Land is one of the most important constraints in the supply of low-cost housing.[23] In Chhattisgarh, such housing is provided mainly by the govern-ment. Government land can be allotted to the Housing Board and if the land is private, it can in the normal course be acquired by compulsory purchase by the District Collector, who is the administrative head of local districts in India, and then allotted to the Housing Board, which will cover the cost. In such cases, change of land-use is automatically approved. The Housing Board does not buy land directly from private parties.

There are many ways in which more land might be made available for low-cost housing.[24] Land policies might in general be made more pro-poor, with secure tenure and clear land titles, and land rights might be clarified. Even if private developers were willing to provide affordable houses, acquir-ing land would be difficult. Considering the rents which tenants can pay, or the selling price of low-cost homes in relation to construction costs, there is only a small margin remaining for the cost of land. As a result, low-cost housing developers either get no land or unattractive sites that other developers do not want (Needham & de Kam, 2000). Developers will naturally build the most profitable type of housing, and this determines the price they will pay for land. If the development of land for low-cost housing is less profitable, it will not be possible for low-cost housing developers to compete in the land market without subsidy or special planning provisions.

The overall scale of the land problem is not overwhelming. One report[25] argues that "not more than 2–3 percent[26] of the total of cities' lands are required to house the existing slum dwelling population in the major metropolitan cities of India" (CEPT, 2010). This report (2010) emphasises that land supply to poorer people is more an issue of appropriate land management tools than of the overall availability of land.

Inclusionary zoning regulations can require developers to make a certain percentage of housing units in new residential developments available to low-income households. In return, developers receive non-monetary compensation – in the form of density bonuses, zoning variances, and expedited permits – that increase their profits in other ways. Such zoning regulations link the production of low-cost homes to private market developers, and thus expand the supply of such homes, which are dispersed throughout an area and thus broaden employment opportunities and foster mixed-income communities. Some zoning policies are mandatory, while others are voluntary or driven by incentives (Policy Link, 2003). Some cities allow the low-cost homes to be built in different locations, or developers may be able to 'buy out' of the rules with a fee instead of building a below-market unit, but the intent and effect of most such inclusionary zoning is to ensure that low-cost units are "included" among the market-rate units (Powell & Stringham, 2005).

Our aim in this book is to discover why the formal private sector does not cater to the low-cost housing market in Raipur. The usual answer – that it is not sufficiently profitable – ignores the institutional structure of markets and how they affect market outcomes. Hence, we argue that if the institutions were different, it is possible that the market outcomes would also be different.

Many actors and institutions are involved in such situations, and their particular structures lead to particular outcomes. The arrangements tend to be both deliberate and accidental, and the outcomes can also be mixed – part intended and part accidental.

Unintended outcomes can be desirable; the actors eventually become aware of the function an institution serves for them and then consciously maintain it, even though its origin was unintended. Similarly, many deliberate institutional arrangements can become less than desirable because of the so-called 'butterfly effect', which means that a seemingly slight variation at the beginning may result in an entirely different outcome from what was intended (Bardhan, 1989), such as the exclusion of low-cost housing.

Institutional structures inevitably acquire some permanence and become resistant to change. In order to change them and to alter their outcomes, their roles and interactions must be examined and analysed, and any changes that are proposed must take account of those interactions. Each actor who is involved – and their interests, their influences on the others, and the outcomes of their interactions – must be identified in order to bring about positive change and improve the regulation of housing provision.

Notes

1 See Ghosh and Sanyal, Muttagi, P.K., Singh, U.B., Sachithanandan, A.N., Thangavel, C., Bhattacharya, K.P., for a collection of essays on Rent Affordability in 'Affordable Housing and Infrastructure in India' (1998); Also see Mascarenhas (2010), Singh S. (2011b), Feedback Ventures (2006), Mahadevia, Joshi, and Sharma (2009), and Mukherji and Bharucha (2011) for more recent data.
2 (ESF/N-AERUS Workshop – Working group 1, 2000).
3 GoCG housing scheme for poor.
4 GoCG housing scheme for very poor households.
5 For Affordable housing in Chhattisgarh, the initial deposit is fixed by the agency that is in charge of the housing project.
6 Which excludes approximately 20% of the families who could not be surveyed, as they reportedly earned higher than the limits set for poor households.
7 11/30 developers.
8 It is more expensive than what is considered affordable housing in this study.
9 Five of the 30 developers who were interviewed had either been a government contractor in the past, were presently working for government, or were considering taking up such assignments.
10 Along with a recurring monthly maintenance fee of Rs. 400 per month.
11 Which excludes approximately 20% of the families who could not be surveyed, as they reportedly earned higher than the limits set for poor households.
12 North here was responding to Demsetz, who posited that institutions evolve so as to produce conditions for steadily increasing economic efficiency. North disagreeing with Demsetz, clarifies that vested interests can prevent movements towards greater economic efficiency.
13 Based on the ancient Roman property law principles (usus, fructus, and abusus).
14 Allen (2000) and Williamson (1993) credit Coase's 1937 paper, 'The Nature of the Firm', for introducing the concept of transaction costs, though he did not use the term.
15 'Capital involved in transforming the physical attributes of a good (i.e., its size, weight, colour, location, chemical composition)'.
16 Even if not of the same magnitude or nature, relating specifically to people on low incomes gaining access to adequate housing.
17 In case of the urban poor in India, democracy offered them a right to vote which they often use in a bargain, to exchange for favours.
18 Mahadevia et al. (2009) andBaken (2003) among others.
19 See NHB Report on Trends & Progress of Housing in India, 2006 for details on the Housing Finance system in India and their Lending Norms.
20 The Alliance of SPARC, NSDF, and MM is currently working with 750,000 households across India and has built or is building housing for over 8500 families.

21 They might also secure private loans, however such loans are usually short term and have a very high interest rate.
22 See Press Trust India (2012), Prasad (2014), Express News Service (2014), and Aiyar (2008)
23 See Needham and de Kam (2000), Robert-Jan Baken (2003), and Kirk (2002)
24 See Payne (2000), Bhadra and Brandao (1993), Atuahene (2004), Benjamin (1999), Barman, Sharma, and Dey (2006), and CEPT, MHUPA-GoI (2010)
25 Mahadevia (2009) India Poverty Report, section 'Land Requirement for Slum Free Cities'. Her extensive study included 25 major cities in India. Except Mumbai, the study claims, in all other cities, the arithmetic of land for rehabilitation of existing slum dwellers accounted for less than 2–3% (in most cases and less than 5% in all cases) of the total land of the city.
26 This is because most slums in India have developed as an urban sprawl. They are not multi-storey dwellings and therefore have low densities even when people are living in cramped housing.

4

WHAT CONSTRAINS
THE DEMAND?

Our interviews with slum dwellers found that more than 70% of the slum households could, if they wish, pay both the initial 20% deposit and the monthly instalments on a house. But just because they have the money to buy a house does not mean that they will do so.

So, what is stopping this potential demand from turning into actual demand?

The survey-based evidence is presented in this chapter, together with anecdotal and personal accounts from the slum dwellers who were gathered through informal discussions. The data provides insight into their present living conditions, their households, their neighbourhoods, and their housing arrangements. It also presents an assessment of their housing needs, their attitude towards their political representatives and the government programmes, and their reasons for staying in the slums. This understanding of how they lead their lives, we hope, will tell us something about the barriers they face in buying such housing.

Who are the residents, and what are
their current housing arrangements?

The residents

Of the 211 households we interviewed, 94 households were very poor and 117 were from the low-income group. One hundred thirty-three of the households had between one and five members in their families, 32% had five to ten members, and 5% had more than ten members. 38% had one earning member, 36% had two earning members, and 26% had three or more. Of the heads of household, 17% were self-employed and 28% were salaried employees, while the majority (55%) were casual labourers or daily wage earners.

The self-employed were petty shopkeepers; small restaurant owners; wedding band musicians; cooks for large events, such as weddings and other social functions; mechanics; ironsmiths; handymen and plumbers; masons; barbers and hair salon owners; laundrymen, street vendors; and local brokers who arrange weddings and land and vehicle deals, and settle disputes for a fee. 28 were salaried employees working for either private or government employers. Those who were employed for private firms worked as cashiers, drivers, security personnel, beauticians, or in retail sales, while those working for the government were employed in the police force, health department, or railways. The majority (55%) were casual labourers; they worked as house help, rickshaw pullers, auto-rickshaw drivers, or construction workers.

Sixty percent of the surveyed families had a bank account and had regular savings; 79% of the surveyed households, including some who did not have a bank account, said that opening or operating a bank account was not a problem for them. Those who found it difficult to cope with paperwork mentioned that bank officials are usually client-friendly and help them with filling in forms and other such formalities. The 40% who did not have bank accounts at the time of the interviews reported either that they had closed their bank accounts and invested their savings elsewhere, or that they had never opened a bank account – either because they did not have enough savings or because they sent all their savings home to support their families back in their villages.

The neighbourhoods

Each slum neighbourhood consisted of different types of housing. Some neighbourhoods had houses built along both sides of a narrow lane, others along a railway track, while some, such as the Lal Ganga Basti, included large open spaces even though they were situated in the middle of the city. Most showed signs of municipal neglect, such as irregular rubbish collection or drains and streets in disrepair. However, such neglect in Raipur is not confined to the slums. Men and women sat on street corners, or under trees, talking. Women sometimes worked in groups, cleaning food grains or combing their children's hair, while men sat in separate groups playing cards or sharing a newspaper with tea.

For the purposes of this survey, the housing structures are broadly divided into three types: *pucca*, or permanent, with walls and roofs made of bricks and concrete; *kaccha*, or temporary, made with makeshift materials; and semi-*pucca*, with brick walls but thatched roofs. While *pucca* homes were relatively well maintained, most semi-*pucca* and *kaccha* homes had health and safety concerns. The distribution of households in our sample between these types was nearly equal.

Forty percent of the surveyed households lived in two-room houses, while 34% lived in one-room houses (Table 4.2). Contrary to what might have been expected, however, the other low-income families were no more likely to live in two-bedroom houses than the poorest people were. The distribution was fairly even and based on factors such as length of stay. In most cases, the second room was an extension of the original structure. When

Figure 4.1 A typical rented house in Gondwara. There were 7 rooms in these, each room rented for Rs. 700. Gondwara, Zone 1, Ward 4

Source: All photographs in this chapter were taken during fieldwork by authors, unless specified otherwise

Figure 4.2 Rented single rooms

Figure 4.3 Another rented home. Each "home" is basically a 10 x 10 sq. ft. area with a corner being demarcated as kitchen and sometimes provided with communal toilets

Figure 4.4 A kaccha home (Veer Shivaji Nagar – Zone 8, Ward 13)

Figure 4.5 A semi-kaccha home (Veer Shivaji Nagar – Zone 8, Ward 13)

Figure 4.6 Kaccha homes with thatched roofs (Veer Shivaji Nagar – Zone 8, Ward 13)

Figure 4.7 Children outside their semi-pucca homes (Srinagar, Gudiyari, Zone 1, Ward 7)

Figure 4.8 Semi-pucca homes (Srinagar, Gudiyari, Zone 1, Ward 7)

Figure 4.9 Outside a semi-pucca home (Srinagar, Gudiyari, Zone 1, Ward 7)

Figure 4.10 A pucca home

Figure 4.11 Another Pucca home, Mahant Talab, Krishna Nagar, Kota (Zone 1, Ward 12)

Table 4.1 Type of housing structure

S. no.	Structure type	Poorest people	Poor people	Total	Percent
1	Pucca	21	47	68	32%
2	Kaccha	37	37	74	35%
3	Semi-pucca	36	33	69	33%
Total		94	117	211	100%

Table 4.2 Number of rooms in the dwelling

S. no.	Number of rooms	Poorest	Low income	Total	Percent
1	One	40	31	71	34%
2	Two	41	44	85	40%
3	Three	7	22	29	14%
4	More than three	6	20	26	12%
Total		94	117	211	100%

there were three or more rooms, usually the family would have been living there for a considerable time and would have demolished the temporary structure and built a new, more permanent structure in its place.

Ninety-eight percent of the surveyed families had electricity in their houses. The remaining 2% used kerosene lamps for lighting. These few households were in different neighbourhoods, and were not all new settlers but people who had not received the *'ekal batti'* (single bulb) connection yet. These homes were often away from the centre of the settlement, so the official electrician would have had a problem – such as having to extend an underground cable – in making the connection to a few houses. In some cases, a connection had been provided but the families had gone back to their villages.

Seventy-three percent of the households used liquified petroleum gas (LPG) for cooking, while the remaining 27% used firewood. Only 15% of the families had access to drinking water within their houses. The remaining 85% used a common tube well or open well or had water delivered by a tanker. Some of the slum dwellers mentioned that the authorities had deliberately prevented them from having access to drinking water pipelines in order to benefit the lucrative water-tanker businesses. They said that bids for tanker routes were awarded as political favours.

Only 37% of the houses had their own toilet facility; 60% had no toilets in their houses, and the families said they had to use open spaces. Women have to wake up very early to relieve themselves, and many families, particularly those with older girls, mentioned this as one of the main reasons they wanted to move out of the slum. The remaining 3% had either built shared toilets or said they used the paid community toilets. The households that had built their own toilets did not have a connection to the sewage system. It was easier to build bathrooms, which could be connected to open drains, than toilets, which need proper solid waste disposal. Nearly 56% had their own bathrooms but only 37% had their own toilets.

Thirty-one percent of the surveyed houses were not connected to any drainage system. The remaining 68% (144 households) had drainage systems which had been provided by the municipality, but in almost every case, the drains were broken. None of the houses in our survey had paved roads; 30% were connected by unpaved roads, while the remaining 70% could only be accessed on foot, or in some cases by a bicycle or a motorcycle.

Sixty-nine percent of the families reported that they had a school within 2 miles of their home, and 68% said that there was a hospital nearby. These were not the same set of households; the Godwara slums are close to a school, but they are far from any hospitals. Similarly, residents of Krishna Nagar and Mantralay Parisar have a hospital nearby, but the schools are far away.

We asked the slum dwellers an open-ended question about what they liked about their neighbourhoods. As shown in Table 4.3. an overwhelming

Table 4.3 Length of stay in the neighbourhood (owner households)

When did you start living in this neighbourhood?	Poorest	Low income	Total	Percent of the owner households	Percent of the total households
0–5 years	2	2	4	2%	2%
5–10 years	7	8	15	8%	7%
10–20 years	17	15	32	18%	15%
20–30 years	26	33	59	32%	28%
More than 30 years	32	40	72	40%	34%
Total	84	98	182	100%	86%

majority did not like anything about their neighbourhood, but about 12% liked the community in the slum, 8% liked its proximity to markets and places of work, and 3% liked the infrastructural services provided in the slum, such as water and electricity.

Land and housing arrangements

Seventy-two percent of the slum dwellers lived without any rights on public land, and 28% were on private land. Seven percent had an occupancy right certificate which had been granted for 30 years by the government in 1998. In an attempt to garner votes, occupancy certificates were awarded to over 2 million slum residents encroaching on government land (Singh N., 1998). Seven and a half percent lived on village land and had no documentation or knowledge of who owned the land. The houses in slums of Gondwara, and parts of Khamardih and Ravigram, appear to be old village houses, and the claimed owners had reportedly been living there for generations. Four householders claimed to have legal title to the land but did not agree to show their records. Some of the people living in these homes were tenants, especially in Gondwara. They were industrial workers in the nearby factories to whom the homeowners had rented part of their property. These rentals were based on informal agreements.

Even if they were on encroached public and private land, the dwelling had sometimes been bought or paid for by the current residents. Thirteen percent of the surveyed families had 'bought' the property that they were living in and were aware that it was an encroached property to which they only had an informal claim. On encroached lands, 72% had built their house using their own materials, while 15% were living in informal rented accommodation. Sixty-two percent had been living in the same slum for more than 20 years. There were few newcomers, and they were mostly renting their homes.

The 86% who were owner-occupiers were generally in a different situation (see Table 4.4). The first group of people who encroached on a piece of land usually built their houses incrementally. A family would come and occupy a certain space within the slum, but as the children grew up the daughters would be married off, and the sons would build new homes, often within the same slum. This probably explains why, even though 62% of the inhabitants had been living in the same neighbourhood for 20 years or more, only 27% were still living in the same house (see Table 4.5). For the same reason, a considerable population (16.5%) had occupied their current homes in the previous five years, while only 2% of them had moved into the neighbourhood in the last five years.

Table 4.4 Length of stay in the current home (owner households)

S. no.	When did you buy/ build this home?	Poorest	Low income	Total	Percent of the owner households	Percent of the total households
1	0–5 years	15	20	35	19%	16.5%
2	5–10 years	21	33	54	29.5%	25.5%
3	10–20 years	17	19	36	20%	17%
4	20–30 years	15	17	32	17.5%	15%
5	More than 30 years	16	9	25	14%	12%
Total owner population		84	98	182	100%	86%

Table 4.5 Cost to build/buy the house

S. no.	Total cost to build/buy the house (1 USD = Rs 75)	Poorest	Low income	Total	Percent
1	Under Rs. 50,000 (< USD 667 approx.)	55	42	97	53%
2	Rs. 50,000–100,000 (USD 667–1334 approx.)	14	27	41	23%
3	Rs. 100,000 to 200,000 (USD 1334–2667 approx.)	7	6	13	7%
4	Rs. 200,000 to 400,000 (USD 2667–5334 approx.)	6	17	23	13%
5	Over Rs. 400,000 (>USD 5334 approx.)	2	6	8	4%
Total		84	98	182	100%

I. Owner occupied

The 182 owner-occupiers who made up 86% of our sample were asked to estimate the cost of their current home. Those whose houses were 30 years old or more were only able to give an approximation of how much it had cost to build, and if they had bought the house, they were asked how much they had paid for it and to give an estimate of its current value. Most owner-occupied houses had cost less than Rs. 100,000, or about 1300 USD, to build or buy, but nearly 15% of the house owners estimated the current value to be between half a million and well over 1 million rupees, or 6700 USD to 13500 USD, while another 10% thought their houses were worth more than 17,000 USD. The figures in Table 4.6 and Table 4.7 exclude about one-fifth of the households who were earning above the official maximum to qualify as belonging to the low-income group.

Table 4.6 Estimation of the current value of the house

S. no.	Estimation of current value (Rs.)	Poorest	Low income	Total	Percent
1	Under 50,000	8	5	13	6%
2	50,000–100,000	15	6	21	10%
3	100,000–200,000	13	23	36	17%
4	200,000–500,000	16	17	33	16%
5	500,000–1,200,000	6	25	31	15%
6	Over 1,200,000	7	14	21	10%
7	Don't know	1	0	1	NA
8	"Nothing now because we have heard rumours that the government is going to clear it."	28	27	55	26%
Total		94	117	211	100%

Table 4.7 House built/bought with credit or savings

S. no.	Built/bought with credit or savings	Poorest	Low income	Total	Percent
1	Credit	17	2	19	11%
2	Savings	31	39	70	38%
3	Savings + credit	30	46	76	42%
4	Sold agricultural land in the village/ sold marriage jewellery/built with compensation money for someone's death or injury	6	11	17	9%
Total		84	98	182	100%

The estimates of house prices were similar across the various slums. The type of structure, whether it was permanent or temporary, and its location – both in terms of where the house was located in the slum, and in which part of the city the slum was located and its access to amenities – determined the house price. A house that was on the main road, even if it was on encroached land, was worth more than a house in the inner parts of the slum. The residents spoke at length about how rumours about certain slums being cleared meant that those houses could not be sold.

Fifty-three percent of households had managed to secure some form of credit for their housing. Anybody with cash to spare could be a moneylender; relatives were often the preferred source for getting a loan. These relatives, however, were often themselves short of money. The borrowers were generally charged 5% simple interest per month so that if they borrowed Rs. 100 this month, then the next month they had to return Rs. 105, if they took two months to return it would be Rs. 110, and so on; this amounts to an annual simple interest rate of 60%. The slum dwellers considered the rate high but fair. They appreciated that the lenders were doing them a favour by lending out their own meagre savings, and at considerable risk. The risk was minimised by keeping the credit to short terms; the informal moneylenders could therefore not lend for longer-term commitments such as buying a house in a formal market.

The slum dwellers also remarked that they often relied on multiple credit sources. For example, if they had taken a loan from the moneylender, they would often borrow from relatives to repay part of the loan.

While nearly 60% of the households had a savings bank account, they did not borrow from banks for housing. Some people said they had taken loans from formal institutions to buy motorbikes or for small business needs, with the help of a guarantor. All of the 103 householders who had taken informal housing loans were aware that banks would demand registration papers and other documents such as proof of identity and address, which they did not possess. The remaining 79 households (37%) had never taken credit for housing.

II. Rental housing

Fourteen percent of our sample, or 29 people, lived in rental housing. Nearly half of them were recent immigrants to the city and had been living there for less than five years, and 90% of them had lived in their house for less than 10 years. Rented houses were either semi-permanent or permanent. The tenants were usually seasonal migrants who came to the city to work as casual labourers during the agricultural off-season. They owned land and houses in the villages where their families lived. The encroachers, who then effectively became owner-occupiers, had usually severed all ties with their villages and had sold any land that they might have owned, in order to bring the whole family with them. They were the more permanent migrants.

Table 4.8 Rents

S. no.	Rents per month	Poorest	Low income	Total	Percent
1	Below Rs. 500/7 USD	0	3	3	10%
2	Rs. 501–1000/7–14 USD	7	9	16	55%
3	Rs. 1001–2000/14–28 USD	3	4	7	25%
4	Above Rs. 2000/28 USD	0	3	3	10%
Total		10	19	29	100%

The monthly rents in 2012 in most slums for a one-room dwelling ranged between Rs. 800 and 1200, or about 12 to 16 USD (see Table 4.8). These houses were typically 100 to 120 square feet, with one corner being used as a kitchen. There were no toilet facilities except in one place in Srinagar with a shared toilet, but some had a partially enclosed section which was used as the bathroom. The rents were increased from time to time, but not on a regular basis. Slightly better-quality houses cost Rs. 100–200 more per month. These were usually occupied by migrants with their wives and children who were still supporting their parents back home, or by people who worked in higher-paid jobs such as drivers or office assistants.

Fifty-five percent of the households had chosen their homes because their relatives lived in the same neighbourhood. The relatives often helped the newcomers to settle in by introducing them to potential employers and landlords. The general opinion among the slum dwellers was that smaller slums were more likely to be cleared, and therefore they often encouraged newcomers from the same villages to live with them in the same neighbourhood.

The remaining 45% of the people in rented accommodations worked on nearby building sites or factories and rented accommodation in adjoining neighbourhoods. Anyone who has a room to spare becomes a landlord. As more migrants arrived, those who had some savings constructed single-room accommodations for them. The landlords explained that these single rooms could be let out to families or as commercial spaces for storage or shops. The landlords usually lived in the same or a nearby slum, and in most cases had already rented out a part of their own house.

Fifty-five percent of the tenants said that in addition to rent, they also paid for repairs and maintenance. The other 45% of tenants had not yet needed to undertake any repairs, and they said that they have had no discussion with their landlord about such issues. Five of them had built extensions on the property, such as a partial enclosure to serve as a bathroom or a plastic sheet over a backyard to serve as an extra bedroom. They said

Table 4.9 Fear of eviction

S. no,	Do you live in constant fear of being evicted?	Poorest	Other low income	Total	Percent
1	Yes	66	77	143	68%
2	No	28	40	68	32%
Total		94	117	211	100%

that minor extensions were tolerated, but their landlords discouraged further encroachments, probably because they posed a possible threat to their informal ownership.

Only two of the tenants had a written rental agreement; the other relationships were based on trust, but they said that if there was any disagreement, the landlord would have the upper hand.

Most of the owner-occupiers and tenants said that one of the biggest drawbacks of living in the slum was the insecurity. They had to invest in some form of housing without any guarantee of its security. 68% of our total sample, or 143 households, admitted that they lived in constant fear of being evicted by the government (see Table 4.9). They mentioned that the insecurity was "always there at the back of their minds", which got worse when there were rumours that their slum might get cleared and receded "when things cooled down".

The remaining 68 households, or 32%, believed that they would not be evicted in the current year because the state legislative elections were drawing near; the threat followed the ebb and flow of state politics. If their elected *Parshad*, or local councillor, did not support them, they would side with the opposing politician, who would be more than willing to help them organise a rally against the elected leader. However, even those who said that they did not live in 'constant fear of being evicted', said that often the thought crossed their minds. So long as the community sticks together, they felt, they would be safe.

What are their housing needs?

We asked our respondents about their housing requirements, in terms of the minimum floor area they believe they need, the location in terms of distance from their current neighbourhood, and preferred amenities.

Ninety percent of our respondents said that they would have no problem with living in a high-rise building, and many of the poorest families were willing to settle for a smaller place if it was of good quality (see Table 4.10).

Nearly all our respondent households indicated that they were willing to 'commute a bit' in order to buy a decent house (see Table 4.11), and 70% were

Table 4.10 Minimum floor area

S. no.	How much would be the minimum floor area for you?	Poorest	Low Income	Total	Percent
1	300 sq. ft.	81	50	131	62%
2	500 sq. ft.	9	63	72	34%
3	500–700 sq. ft.	4	4	8	4%
Total		94	117	211	100%

Table 4.11 Distance consideration for the new house

S. no.	If so, how far would you be willing to move from the current location?	Poorest	Low income	Total	Percent
1	1–2 km	6	6	12	6%
2	5–6 km	23	20	43	21%
3	10–12 km	31	56	87	43%
4	Anywhere in Raipur within 5 km of the city limits	26	33	59	30%
Total		86	115	201	100%

ready to move as far as 10–12 kilometres from their current location. Many of them who lived in the periphery of the city mentioned that while they would be willing to move even further than 10–12 kilometres, the distance was less important than the actual place to which they were going. They were willing to move in any direction as long as it was within 5–6 kilometres of the city limits, because easy access to the city was their primary consideration.

Nearly 70% of the surveyed households agreed that having better public transport would help immensely. The 30% who were against public transport were mainly rickshaw or auto-rickshaw drivers who feared it would damage their livelihood.

Eighty percent of our sample said that a mid-rise dwelling with five basic amenities – drinking water, toilet, electricity, drainage, and roads – would be adequate for their needs. On being asked if they felt they had any other requirements, they were quite realistic in their assessment of what they could afford. Some said "if I dream of the moon, I won't get it", and others who were more resigned to their fate jokingly replied that the mosquitoes in the slums did not let them sleep, let alone have dreams, so all they could afford to do was live one day at a time rather than build castles in the air.

About one-fifth of the respondents felt that it was vital to live near to social amenities such as public markets, schools, hospitals, a police station, parks, parking, and workshop space. They feared that if they bought homes without such amenities, the authorities and builders would forget about them but the majority of social amenities would develop gradually, and 15% of respondents mentioned that they currently had space around the house where they kept livestock such as poultry and that they would prefer a similar facility in any new house.

What barriers do they face in buying a home?

The slum dwellers had many different difficulties in buying a home. Before starting the survey, we organised an informal group discussion in the Gandhi Nagar slum, where our study assistant lived. About 20 people took part. The discussion started with around 25 people, but some left and others joined as it went on. The group was told about the estimated costs that they might incur in buying a home. They were asked to raise their hands if they thought any of the residents of the slum, their neighbours and themselves included, would be able to afford such a house, without naming them.

A few people raised their hands, and they were then asked what they thought stopped people from buying such a home. They said that there were no suitable homes available, that it would take too long to find a home, that they could not raise the necessary finance, they would not be trusted, or they would not be able to find a guarantor. It was also suggested that the available houses were too small or badly built and that the necessary formalities were too cumbersome, and the officials would have to be bribed.

The problems listed by the participants in the group discussion served as the checklist for the household survey. Each respondent was asked whether he or she personally agreed that the constraint was a barrier to securing an affordable home. They were also asked if they had any more constraints to add to the list.

The list of constraints was discussed by slum households irrespective of their capacity to pay. Some households – but not all – who said that they could not afford a 'model house' dropped out of the survey after answering questions about their current housing conditions and capacity to pay. Only 201 households answered the constraints section.

The issue of trust was split into two in order to get more detailed information. Respondents were asked to agree or disagree with two different statements: "*I have heard of people getting cheated*" and "*It happened to me, I got cheated*". Only 28 households said that they themselves had been victims of fraud in informal real estate dealings, whereas the perceived lack of trust was more widespread. The constraints and the number of households who agreed with them are listed in Table 4.12 and are indicated in brackets.

77

Table 4.12 Demand constraints – ranked according to the number of people who agreed with the constraint

Demand constraints		Poorest	Poor	Total
What is stopping you from buying low-cost homes in the formal market?	Total number of households who answered this part of the survey	86	115	201
1) Non-availability of formal low-cost homes on the private market	Number of households who agreed with the constraint	86	115	201
2) House-hunting is a very time-consuming process		70	113	183
3a) Trust issues – "I have heard of people being cheated."		65	112	177
4) Lack of access to long-term, cheap credit		74	98	172
5) The registration process is cumbersome, and bribes make it expensive		66	99	165
6) Lack of a third-party guarantor		40	75	115
7) The houses are too small for our families		25	51	76
8) The houses are of poor quality		5	27	32
3b) Trust issues – "I was myself the victim of a fraud."		9	19	28

Some affordable housing is provided by the government within the city limits. There are not enough of these houses to satisfy the demand, and they are not openly available for sale but are allocated in a lottery. The number of applications for these houses is much greater than the number of houses available, and the screening for eligibility is a lengthy process. The Housing Board has even had to call in the police to control the crowds who queue up to file their applications. The number of eligible applicants is far higher than the number of houses available, and hence, the housing is allotted with a lottery. If a large family, such as two brothers living together with their families, need and can afford two adjoining houses, they cannot buy them because of the lottery allotment.

There are about 125,000 households in Raipur who live in slums, and the government has been able to build no more than 5000 dwellings a year (Interviewee-3F). At this rate it would take 25 years to house all the slum households even if the population were to remain constant, whereas it is actually growing rapidly.

Many respondents said that house-hunting was a time-consuming process; if they spent too much time on it, they risked not only losing their wages for the day but also their jobs. Self-employed vendors would lose their vending spaces and their customers, apart from the loss of income. Over 90% of the respondent households said this was an issue. They said that if there were enough homes, it would not be so time-consuming to find one.

A hundred and seventy-seven of the 201 households had heard of people being cheated and losing their entire life savings when trying to buy a house. Twenty-eight of them had themselves actually lost money in land and housing deals. While respondents may or may not have actually been cheated by the formal developers, they perceive real estate dealings as risky, which discourages them from buying houses in the open market. Slum dwellers engage in informal land deals, and often get cheated, or hear of such stories. They realise that such dealings are not legal, but they continue to engage in them, partly because some people in the neighbourhood seem to be profiting from them, and partly because they are deceived by clever salesmanship. These salespeople are said to frequent the neighbourhood tea shops and other places and talk to gullible slum dwellers, convincing them to part with their savings in fake property deals.

However, while the slum dwellers realise that not every land deal is similarly informal and risky, they do not have much faith in the formal system either. If something were to go wrong, they feel that they lack the wherewithal and the confidence to support their claims in a court of law. Possession of a certified document does not always provide them with the necessary sense of security about their investments. However, in a general sense, the slum dwellers seemed to trust the government and are not averse to investing in a government project. While, in the opinion of the slum dweller, the government may not build enough homes or provide all the infrastructure as promised, they were confident that they would be given the keys to the home that they have invested in.

Eighty-five percent, or 172, of our respondents mentioned that their lack of access to low-cost formal credit was a major problem, and 115 mentioned the need for a third-party guarantor. Most slum dwellers have access to short-term, informal loans which cost around 60% per annum and are therefore unsuitable for financing a house on the formal market. When people said they lacked 'cheap credit', they were not referring to subsidised loans but to ordinary formal housing loans, which cost around 8% to 12% per year.

Most slum dwellers cannot get formal loans because they do not have the required proof of identity and formal addresses; slum houses do not have postal addresses, and government departments have their own systems for identifying slum houses, such as codes or numbers painted on the walls or doors, which are used when the slums are being surveyed.

Many slum dwellers did not possess basic identification documents. They all had voter IDs and/or driving licences, but their names were often incorrect or inconsistent. Most dwellings had only the ward number as their address;

for example, every household in the Fafadih slum of Kali Nagar had the same address on their voter ID. Even the slum dwellers who had bank accounts, and also had the relevant documents such as a bank passbook or driver's licence, did not satisfy the requirements for credit. They needed to have proof of their identity and their address, which required utility bills that they did not have.

Some banks require a third-party guarantor, which is difficult for slum dwellers. If someone who qualifies is buying a house that has been officially provided by the government for poorer people, the Housing Board acts as a third-party guarantor. If a household wants to buy from a private builder, they are unlikely to be able to find a guarantor.

Over 80% of the households believed that the registration process was expensive and bureaucratic, although less than 1% of them were aware of the actual cost of registration. They were also unaware that registration is free for the poorest families. When they were told about this, almost every family had the same answer: It was not only the actual fee that was a problem, but bribes had to be paid to every party involved in the process. It was difficult to ascertain how much they thought it would cost. But their estimates of the cost of getting a property registered ranged from Rs. 10,000–50,000, or between 150 USD and 700 USD.

Most respondents were aware that they had to get a housing plan approved, and that they had to make the rounds of various government departments to get their documents approved. They did not have information about the kind of documents that would be required, but they feared that they would not have what was needed. 38% of the households in our sample considered a 300-square-foot dwelling too small. They explained that their current homes on encroached land were much larger, and even if the house is small, they can make use of the space in front of it as an extended living space. Living in a multi-storeyed house would not allow them to do this.

Sixteen percent of our respondents mentioned Kabir Nagar, a Housing Board project where the houses had collapsed while they were being built; they were afraid that private builders compromised on the quality of affordable homes. They also mentioned that if they had any disagreement with a builder, they would not stand a fair chance. If they did buy a house on the open market, they were sure they would probably get a bad deal. Also, they feared that without their community's support, their demands for water connections or other services might be promised but not necessarily delivered.

This fear is not baseless. The only houses built in the formal sector for poorer people are built by the government. Corruption aside, these houses are usually far from what is promised. The government departments who built the houses had no details on how often the houses were left unfinished, but according to the slum dwellers, this often happened. The slum dwellers are reluctant to move into an unfinished house, partly because it is difficult

Figure 4.12 Government-provided homes into which it was expected slum dwellers would move

Source: PRIA. (2012, October 3). "Poor Living" for the Urban Poor – tracing JNNURM housing projects. Terra Urban. Raipur: Participatory Research in Asia (PRIA). http://terraurban.wordpress.com/tag/jnnurm/

to get the work completed once the house is occupied but mainly because they fear that once they move in, the builders will not complete any of the remaining tasks.

Our informal discussions with the slum dwellers showed that even if they were willing and able to buy, they would not necessarily themselves be willing to move out of the slum. Most slum dwellers considered that any new house they could buy would be an investment and a safety net. They would buy such a home if it was available, rent it out, and continue living in the slum. Then, if and when the slum was cleared, they would not miss the entitlement for a free home. The 'hope of a free home' was an incentive to stay in the slum and not move out but did not affect their willingness to buy if it was possible. There was always a possibility that some of the evicted slum dwellers would not get replacement homes, and in such cases, they would need a shelter.

While these households regarded a decent 300–500 square feet apartment with a toilet, running water, electricity, roads, and drainage to be value for money, they were worried about changing their lifestyle. Almost 10% of the sample said that they would not move into a high-rise apartment, irrespective of whether they could afford it, and eight households said that they needed a minimum of between 500–700 square feet.

There were several reasons why our respondents valued living in a slum. Many of them pointed out that their strength lay in their unity. Most of the people in a given slum had generally migrated from the same village. In the case of the Bhawna Nagar slum, for instance, the first occupant to come there narrated how she had managed to convince other people from her village to come and encroach on adjoining lands, in order to provide her with support. Many of the people who said that they could buy their own decent housing, pointed out that their neighbours might not be able to join them. When asked why this was important, their answers ranged from practical difficulties such as losing childcare, to more emotional issues such as the loss of friends and community solidarity.

This was not superficial; such issues are vital in the slums. While younger men and women go to work, their children usually play in the neighbourhood under the watchful eyes of the older men and women. They also knew that if they needed services in their neighbourhood, such as getting a hand pump installed or getting streetlights, they needed to be united if they were to convince their local councillor or *Parshad*. It was less attractive to buy a new house in an apartment block without community support.

What they wanted was to have a house with a legal title that they could sell if need be, or which would serve as an investment if they did not need to live in it themselves. Our respondents' anxiety for options may have been caused by the slum clearances which were going on in Raipur at the time of our interviews. There may also have been some element of strategic bias – people responded in ways which they thought might encourage favourable policies.

Slum clearances lead to insecurity, but slum upgrading programmes such as the Rajiv Awas Yojana (RAY), where the government provides basic facilities, have the opposite effect. It was believed that security of tenure was a necessary condition for people to invest in their own housing and infrastructure, but later slum upgrading programmes tend to use infrastructure investment in order to enhance the security of tenure and to encourage housing investment. People who earn significantly more than the limit for the poorest category and would be able to pay to move out but have already invested considerable sums in their slum homes are the most reluctant to move out. These people are often politically connected and are influential in the community. One of the most serious drawbacks to the provision of replacement homes for slum dwellers is that governments in India, or indeed worldwide, cannot remotely afford to upgrade the homes of even 100 million people, and this is only about 10% of the world's total slum population. Slum upgrading does, however, create a 'hope value'; slum dwellers like to believe that, in time, they will have access to a clean environment with basic amenities. This very natural reluctance to move is the result of government policies.

Conclusion

We have argued that some of the poorest and low-income people in Raipur, with their existing incomes and the level of costs, would be able to afford decent low-cost homes if the institutional arrangements were different. Taking even the most conservative figures, more than 50% of our respondents said that they would be able to buy their own low-cost homes, if the various problems that discouraged them were addressed. About one-fifth of the slum population was not included in the survey, as they said that their earnings were above the official low-income limits. If these households are also included, approximately 70% of the slum population would be financially able to buy their own homes. The better-off one-fifth of the slum population, particularly in the slums of Khamardih, Telibandha, Mahant Talab, Srinagar, and Behra Para who were not part of the survey, might not be willing to buy such homes as they have already built permanent houses in the slum, as is shown in the photographs of the three types of housing.

Our survey of 201 slum dwellers showed that while credit was one major demand constraint, there were other constraints such as the lack of suitable homes, the lack of trust, the belief that house-hunting would take a lot of time, and bureaucratic hurdles. Our survey also showed that some slum dwellers considered that it might be better not to move out of the slum, in the hope that government slum clearance programmes might possibly provide them with a free or cheap dwelling elsewhere sometime in the future.

5

WHAT CONSTRAINS THE SUPPLY?

When we interviewed our sample of 30 out of a total of 70 registered developers in Chhattisgarh, we attempted to avoid any preconceptions or suggestions as to what we felt were the main constraints to the supply of affordable housing. We used a fairly informal approach of semi-structured interviews, and no suggestions or pre-prepared list of constraints were asked for or provided.

The developers were asked to list all the issues that discouraged them from entering the affordable housing market. They were then asked to indicate those they found to be critical, and these are the constraints listed in Table 5.1. The 'critical' constraints were those that developers said actually prevented them from entering the market. There was no restriction on the number of constraints they could identify as critical.

The developers were asked to rate each of the constraints they identified on a scale of 1 to 10, 10 being the most serious. They were encouraged to be realistic and were asked to justify the ratings, thereby reducing the risk of random ratings. They were also reassured, before and during the interview, that their identities would be kept anonymous if they wished.

The ratings in Table 5.1 are the average of all 30 developers whom we interviewed, and the list indicates all of the constraints they mentioned during the interviews. The ratings were not weighted by the size of the developer, but the averages are affected by the numbers of developers who mentioned the constraints as well as their view of the constraints' seriousness. In most cases, however, the ratings were quite consistent,[1] perhaps because developers in Chhattisgarh had at the time been actively lobbying against "constraining regulations".

The developers seemed to be aware of the opportunities available if a low-cost housing market develops and of the factors that constrain them from supplying it, and they were also aware of the discussions on the topic at the state and national levels. During the course of the fieldwork, for instance, the state government organised a workshop on 'Housing for all', which came up with five recommendations to lower the cost of housing. Our questionnaire was amended to include questions on those recommendations, but

Table 5.1 Supply constraints rated

List of constraints	Rating on a scale of 1–10 (10 being the most critical)	Constraint mentioned in how many interviews	Mean	Standard deviation
Non-availability of low-cost land	9.43	30	9.31	1.33
Slow government approval process	6.43	25	7.86	1.92
Lack of access to credit for low-income buyers	5.57	22	7.27	2.17
Double taxation (industry and service tax) & high approval cost due to bribes	3.43	13	7.77	1.55
Construction cost dependent on market fluctuations	1.83	11	5.50	2.16
Low permitted floor to area density ratio	1.83	6	7.44	2.35
No infrastructure, transport, or connectivity	1.43	8	9.10	1.16
Labour shortage due to government anti-poverty schemes and food subsidies	1.13	7	5.75	2.75
Government supply of affordable housing lowers market price	1.00	3	10.00	0
Non-availability of institutional credit at low interest rates to developers	0.93	4	6.69	2.44
The government allots low-cost homes, they are not allowed to be sold on the open market	0.73	3	7.05	2.51

our results showed that the lack of available land, the difficult government approval process, and potential buyers' lack of credit were clearly the most pressing. The non-critical constraints were compiled into a separate list as 'issues but not constraints', which is contained in Table 5.2.

The developers were also asked about the extent to which a particular constraint had to be addressed before they would consider entering the low-cost housing market; for instance, 'By how much would taxes have to be reduced before you would enter this market?', or 'By how much would the cost of land have to be reduced, before you would enter the market?'. The constraints are analysed in the order of their importance as suggested by the developers.

Table 5.2 Issues but not constraints

S. no.	Issues but not constraints	Number of developers who mention the issue	Percent
1	Land laws/administrative reforms needed [these include issues other than the approval process]: Change of land use to be permitted, land records and cadastral systems improved and computerised. Better qualified personnel at Patwari levels who can work on GIS maps.	28	93.33
2	CGHB is a market player with added benefits and should not itself be in the market. They distort the market.	19	63.33
3	The 15% land reservation for poorer people housing is unfair for the developer.	16	53.33
4	There is no separate policy on affordable housing, so we are not sure what to expect.	10	33.33
5	Labour shortages because of government make-work schemes have impacted work ethics.	7	23.33
6	There is less social acceptance for mixed housing where the rich and poor have the use of the same common amenities.	6	20.00
7	The present allotment process in the homes for the poor.	5	16.67
8	Low-income groups have a tendency to hold protests rather than take legal recourse, which is bad PR. There is a need for institutions to protect the developers.	5	16.67

1 Non-availability of low-cost serviced land

Unserviced land on the outskirts of the city is available at affordable prices, but invariably, such land would require considerable investment in services. Having made such an investment, the developers would naturally construct the type of housing which would make the most profit. The developers made it clear that the price of the land should not be so high that the developer has to reduce the quality of construction.

The developers also pointed out that location is important for low-income people; they need to live near government schools, shops, open space, public transport, and workplaces such as high-end residential complexes and markets. If a developer cannot provide housing in such an area, then the buyers will not be interested.

On-site infrastructure development, such as internal roads, drainage, gardens, and street lighting, is undertaken by the developers. The developers considered that off-site development, such as connecting roads, electrification, municipal water pipelines, and developing drainage services to which developers could connect their internal drainage systems, should be undertaken by the government.

Most developers were of the opinion that instead of creating new suburbs and developing infrastructure on the outskirts, a faster and cheaper solution would be land pooling in the existing slums, or by letting the developers build and sell low-cost homes on 15% of land that they are presently obliged to reserve for poorer people. Generally, however, the developers agreed that better town planning was needed to make land available.

Land pooling involves the assembly of several small plots of land into a large plot, and the provision of infrastructure. The serviced land is then returned to the original owners, less a certain amount which is sold by whatever agency has led the initiative, in order to cover the cost of the infrastructure and services. The original landowners thus obtain plots within the reshaped area which are rather smaller in size than what they had before, but they gain from having access to infrastructure and services (UN-ESCAP, 1998). This unique approach to the resolution of slum eviction conflicts requires strong community organisation, a formal and binding agreement, substantial densification into smaller plots, and some reconstruction and capital investment, either from residents' savings or loans from outside (Angel & Boonyabancha, 1988; Hong & Needham, 2007).

In India, if land is acquired under the Right to Fair Compensation and Transparency in Land Acquisition, Rehabilitation and Resettlement (RFCT-LARR) Act, 2013, the government is required to pay close to four times the market value for rural land and twice for urban areas. As a result, land pooling has emerged as a viable alternative; private land is transferred to the authority in charge, and the pooled parcels of land are then developed by the authority, with some part being used for common development. The remaining land is then sectioned off and returned to the original landowners in the same proportion as their original property.

The developers claimed that uncertainty about the availability of land forced them to build in higher profit margins so that they could buy land for future projects; they implied that they could operate on lower profit margins if land availability was assured. While the developers largely blamed the government for pushing up housing prices because the 15% reservation makes land more costly for the majority of the upper-middle class, who do not benefit from it, they admitted that land hoarding and speculation by landowners and other construction firms also played a central role in increasing prices.

2   Slow government approval process

The eight stages of the government approval process, starting with registration, were said to take between 8 and 26 months, as shown in Table 5.3.
This was confirmed by all 30 developers. They agreed that developers who
were politically connected, who had their papers in order, or who had more
money to spend on bribes or on staff to visit and wait outside government
offices, could get the approvals in about 18 months, while some of the
smaller developers who lacked these resources could only get approvals in
about 26 months.

Only the first two steps in the approval process – registration and
mutation – are covered by the World Bank report (World Bank, 2009).
Developers, however, have to go through a minimum of six more steps
before they can start construction. These steps are defined in Table 5.4.
We have partly simplified the language to save space, but the terminology
should serve to show the complex and tortuous nature of the procedures.

Table 5.4 should convey some of the complexity of the procedures, and
each of the many transactions takes time and may need to be appropriately
'lubricated'. In addition, high-rise blocks[2] need permission from the High
Rise Committee. Each of these steps involves several sub-steps. For example,
Town and Country Planning approval includes 26 points which have to be
approved by nine separate departments.

Delays in approvals cause many problems. They cause extra costs
in terms of interest accrued on money paid for land and for bribes,
and the time required to make multiple visits to the various offices.

Table 5.3 Timeline required for the government approvals in Chhattisgarh

S. no.	Process	Office	Time taken
1	Land registration	Office of the Registrar	1–2 days
2	Change in land use	Office of the Tehsildar	1 month
3	Demarcation	Office of the Patwari	4 months
4	Layout approval	Town and Country Planning Unit	6 months – 1 year (sometimes more)
5	Diversion	Court of the Sub Divisional Officer (Revenue)	1–4 months
6	Nazul No Objection Certificate (NoC)	Nazul division	1–4 months (Diversion and Nazul process can run in parallel)
7	Colony development permission	Municipality	4–6 months
8	Building approval	Zonal office	2 months

Table 5.4 The approval process

S. no.	Process	Office	Process defined
1	Land registration	Office of the District Registrar (or Sub-Registrar)	The office records deeds of any transaction, including transactions relating to land and real estate. The execution of the sale deed in front of the two witnesses is conducted by the office of the Sub Registrar of Assurances within whose jurisdiction the property is located. The registration is evidence of a transaction, and the document alone is not equivalent to the land title.
2	Mutation (change of name)	Court of the Tahasildar/ Office of the Revenue Inspector	Section 110 of the Chhattisgarh Land Revenue Code, 1959. Section 109 requires that anyone acquiring any interest in land to report to the officials within six months. The Court of the Tahasildar passes orders on an application by the buyer of land for mutation (change) of title in his name in the Field Book maintained under the Chhattisgarh Land Revenue Code, 1959. Acting on the orders of the Court of Tahsildar, the Revenue Inspector instructs the Patwari to enter the change in the Field Book. The Patwari does this and issues a fresh extract of the Field Book bearing the name of the person who has acquired the right.
3	Demarcation	Court of the Tahasildar or Office of the Revenue Inspector (RI), and Patwari	The Patwari is a field worker who ensures that every landholder having lands adjoining a village road, village waste, or land reserved for communal purposes, demarcates his land at his own cost. The Patwari marks the boundaries of their landholding, in the presence of witnesses from the village who generally are the 'elders' of the village.
4	Layout approval	Office of the Assistant Director (or Director), Town and Country Planning (T&CP)	The T&CP unit prepares and notifies a Master Plan for the town, to ensure that the proposed development is in conformity with the Master Plan in terms of land use and floor area ratio.

(Continued)

Table 5.4 (Continued)

S. no.	Process	Office	Process defined
5	Diversion	Court of the Sub Divisional Officer (Revenue)	If a landowner desires to 'divert' agricultural land to a nonagricultural use, they require prior permission of the SDO (Revenue). The rate of land revenue is according to the land use. If a landowner wants to divert the land use from farming to housing or industrial, it must first be 'diverted' by the SDO (Revenue) through a revenue court process. This ensures that the new land use is in the public interest. Even when land is marked as residential in the Master Plan, it is not automatically considered so for tax purposes. Therefore, diversion has to be done. A reform for 'automatic diversion' of urban land according to land use in a Master Plan is currently being considered in Chhattisgarh.
6	Nazul NOC	Office of the Nazul Officer	"Nazul land" is government land in a municipality which has not been bought by another party. The Nazul Officer maintains the record of government land in municipal areas and must issue a 'no objection certificate' before development by a private entity, to confirm that it is not Nazul land.
7	Colony development permission	Municipal Office (in urban areas), and Sub Divisional Magistrate (SDM) in rural areas including development areas.	The municipality controls development of any land in the municipal area. 'Development' refers to dividing a parcel of land into plots, and creation of infrastructure such as roads and drainage. Development of a new 'colony' includes internal infrastructure and external development, which is done outside the colony's area, to link it to the trunk services of the town. Internal development must be completed before building permission can be granted, and the developer has to pay a certain amount to the municipality depending on the area and the type of housing society.

(Continued)

S. no.	Process	Office	Process defined
8	Building control	Municipal Office	In terms of Section 293 of the Chhattisgarh Municipal Corporation Act, 1956, any erection or re-erection or extension of a building requires prior permission of the Commissioner. Building permission is granted for colonies only after the internal development works are complete.

Bharucha (2013) states that the cost of bribes in smaller cities was around Rs. 65, or 1 USD, per square foot, while in Mumbai it could be as much as Rs. 500, or almost 7 USD. It was said that even the basic civic clearances for a small plot in Dadar in Mumbai would apparently cost about Rs. 4 million, or about 55,000 USD. Such a cost may be bearable for higher-income housing, but it can make low-income housing totally unaffordable.

Seven of our respondent developers claimed that further delays and costs arise from the need to bribe lower-level bureaucrats. The layout approval is given for the entire project, but the building permission is granted in stages, as government officials make intermittent checks to ensure that the building is being constructed in accordance with the plan. Such checks, the developers complained, were unnecessary; they said that one check only should be made, after the project has been completed. These intermittent checks were reported to cause considerable delays, as construction would have to be stopped for each check and contractors would have to be re-engaged after the inspector had cleared the project to continue. The contractor, meanwhile, might find other work elsewhere, which would further delay the process and would provide further opportunities for bribes to the government officials.

Around one-third of our developer respondents stated that corruption was a problem, but they considered that the problems arose from a variety of issues such as bureaucratic hurdles, resistance to change, red tape, too many different departments, and most importantly, the shortage of staff.

3 Low-income buyers' lack of access to credit

Potential buyers' lack of access to mortgage finance was agreed to be an important problem, which decreased the effective demand. Our respondent developers believed that there was probably enough demand from low-income buyers to sustain their businesses for 10 years. In addition, almost all developers have their own finance schemes, under which buyers lose their houses if they fail to pay the agreed instalments. The demand is so high that the developers do not have any problem reselling properties if buyers default.

These schemes are especially suitable for rather better-off clients, such as small business owners and truck drivers, who can afford the instalments but do not have the documents needed to secure a formal mortgage loan.

4   Dual taxation and high approval cost due to bribes

The construction sector is currently listed under both 'industry' and 'service sector' for taxation purposes. Hence, construction firms have to pay industrial taxes as well as an additional 12% service tax.

Developers' opinions were divided on the importance of this issue. Thirteen said it was one of the more important constraints, but the other 17 developers did not mention it. They said that even if taxes were lowered, they would still not be able to enter the low-cost housing market unless the constraints of land, delayed approvals, and credit were resolved. They were clear that if those constraints were resolved, they might be able to enter the market with the existing levels of taxes.

Other developers believed that taxes are unduly heavy for the construction industry when compared to other sectors. Every year, a new form of tax is introduced – VAT, Service Tax, and Excise tax – along with a new department to collect it. More has to be spent on the taxes, as well as on bribes for each different department. High taxes and bribes were therefore grouped together as one supply constraint, as many developers feel that they are directly linked to each other.

5   No control on escalation of construction cost

Developers estimate the costs of a project before they start construction, and they make an allowance for minor fluctuations in costs. However, delays in the approvals mean that the price estimates are no longer valid because of increases in the prices of raw materials and the cost of construction. This makes it especially difficult to plan and execute low-cost housing projects. In high-end markets, cost increases can normally be passed on to the buyer, but low-cost home buyers need fixed prices. Cost increases can be reduced if the delays between the initial plan and actual construction can be estimated and reduced.

6   Low permitted floor-to-area ratio – density measure

The floor-to-area ratio (FAR) regulates the maximum ratio of a building's total floor area to the area of the land upon which it is built. The ratio in Raipur ranges from 1–1.5 within the city, to 2 in some areas in the outskirts. When the ratio is 2, the highest permitted number of floors is five, plus the ground floor which is usually used for parking. According to our developers, this is very low for a densely populated and fast-growing city. A higher ratio would allow more dwelling units to be built on a given area of land, which would reduce the effect of the high cost of land. However, it is likely that the cost of land would increase if the ratio is increased, unless the land had been bought long before the ratio was changed.

7   Lack of social infrastructure and transport

Newly developed areas lack schools, markets, hospitals, and police stations. All 30 developers complained that government money was spent on building affordable housing rather than providing the infrastructure which would enable developers to do so. This constraint was not rated among the most serious problems because the developers assumed that, if it becomes profitable to build low-cost homes, social amenities will come up in due course. Six percent of the land in each colony in Chhattisgarh is reserved for commercial development. This usually consists of a row of small grocery shops, pharmacies, beauty salons, and eateries along the colony's periphery, which usually rely on business from the colony. Generally, auto-rickshaws, private schools, and private hospitals compensate for the lack of public services.

8   Labour shortage due to government anti-poverty schemes and food subsidies

Government and private developers face shortages of skilled labourers. CREDAI estimated that there was a shortage of 12 million skilled workers in the construction sector in India (Iyer, 2012). This causes an erratic supply of labour, and hence further delays, which ultimately increase the cost of construction. This also affects developers' ability to achieve economies of scale and mass-produce low-cost homes because construction work generally depends on manual labour rather than on machines.

Our developers said that labour shortages are worse because of government schemes in Chhattisgarh. The state provides heavily subsidised food grains to low-income families for as little as 2 rupees a kilo, or a little over 1 cent a pound. The availability of labour is also reduced by the Mahatma Gandhi National Rural Employment Guarantee Act (MG-NREGA), which aims to reduce migration by providing work in rural areas. Most construction workers are migrants or daily commuters from the villages, and this programme enables them to secure work in their villages without having to travel farther from home. One developer said that these two programmes have turned good workers into lazy villagers.

Seven of our 30 developers said that the labour shortage was a minor issue rather than a major constraint, because they believed that the construction industry would soon use more machinery, so that their dependence on manual labour would be reduced.

9   Government supply of low-cost housing lowers its price

The local authority Housing Board builds low-cost housing and, as a government agency, enjoys certain privileges such as subsidised land, certain exemptions from statutory requirements, and a slightly smoother and faster approval process. They also sell the homes at cost; all this allows them to sell dwellings at prices lower than a commercial developer could. The Board also liaises with other government agencies to provide subsidies from other schemes, so that the houses are usually sold substantially below the 'market price'. This, the developers believe, is a potential risk for them, as the buyers will not be interested in buying a similar home for a higher price.

Of the 30 developers, 11 said that unless the Board limited its sales to those who could probably never afford to buy at the market price – such as households that in 2012 were earning below around Rs. 5000, or about 70 USD, per month – then those who were better off would never be willing to pay a higher price for a house built commercially, because there was always a possibility that they might get a subsidised house from the Board.

The other 19 developers considered this to be an issue but not an important constraint. They argued that if the major constraints such as land, approvals, credit, and infrastructure were addressed so that developers could profitably construct low-cost homes, the government would not pose serious competition as it supplies only a fraction of the demand.

10   Non-availability of institutional credit at low interest rates to developers

Developers have to pay 15% to 18% interest on business loans; some say that this limits their ability to supply low-cost homes. They start building these homes as soon as they get the necessary approvals. Potential buyers then apply to the bank that is associated with the project for a personal home loan, but not all homes get sold at the launch of the project. If there is any delay in the supply of funds, the cost increases and the developers have to get loans from private financers at interest rates which they say are "high" but less than the banks' rates. This is a problem for all types of housing, but it is a constraint to the low-cost housing market because the extra cost can make the houses unaffordable.

11   Low-cost homes are allotted, and their open sale is not allowed

Low-cost houses in Chhattisgarh, whether built by the government or by private developers, have to be allotted by the District Collector, and the government sets the price. When a new low-cost home development is launched, the developers call for applications, which are then scrutinised by a government committee that is set up for the process. The committee selects the individuals by a lottery, and then finalises the list for allotment. As with all government bureaucratic processes, there are many delays in this. Five of the respondent developers believed that if there was a free market for low-cost homes, the government might consider scrapping the allotment process.

Developers' perception of the government

After the discussion about these constraints, the developers were asked some additional questions about their views of government and the rules. They perceived the rules to be unfair and unjustified and the authority to be illegitimate. They believe the whole government system to be rent-seeking, corrupt, and inefficient, and that there is no clarity of purpose or coordination among the various departments. They mistrusted the government bureaucrats and politicians and were generally reluctant to deal with the government. When asked if they would prefer the government to act as an intermediary, buying houses and selling them to families under some sort of guarantee, they generally felt that it would be good to have a guarantee but they would rather not deal with the government at all.

The developers feel that the government's efforts to deal with the shortage of houses have been inadequate, as half of Raipur's population lives in slums. The Chhattisgarh Government Housing Board is the main provider of low-cost homes, and the role of private developers and other related government agencies – such as the Raipur Development Authority and the Raipur Municipal Corporation – is considered largely to be a supplement to the efforts of CGHB. The developers believe that this leads to poor coordination and duplication of effort, where every government agency associated with housing comes up with new subsidised house building schemes for low-income people, instead of helping developers to supply what is needed. They argue that the government's preoccupation with building low-cost homes itself, instead of facilitating private developers to do so, has led to serious neglect of the need for urban infrastructure.

The developers also complained about the lack of discussion of issues such as better town planning, low-cost building methods, taxation, and labour shortages. Currently, town planners in Chhattisgarh cannot allocate land separately for the different segments of the housing market. This issue is partially solved by inclusionary zoning, where developers reserve land and housing for low-income groups. The Urban Local Bodies (ULBs) are tasked to acquire the land, by paying the registered cost of land to the developer. The registered cost is the amount that is paid at the time of registration. However, they do not have the funds they would need to carry out this function, so this land reservation, the developers claim, is only on paper; the land becomes no-man's land because the developers are not allowed to develop it, and the government lacks the resources to acquire it.

Table 5.5 Questions about developers' perception of the government

Questions and answers	Number of developers who agreed (out of 30)	Percent
Do you think the government is aware of the constraints to low-cost housing development? Yes	30	100
Is it easy to address these constraints? Yes	13	43.3
Is it easy to address these constraints? No	17	56.6
Which part of government should address these constraints?		
1. The Municipality/Nagar Nigam head/ Town and Country Planning Unit/ Raipur Development Authority	8	26.6
2. Ministry of Housing and Environment + Urban Development at the national level and their respective Secretaries	13	43.3
3. Chief Minister	9	30
Why are these issues not being addressed?		
1. Bureaucratic hurdles/resistance/red tape/difficult to change government processes/too many departments control this sector/inadequate staff	11	36.6
2. Government lacks vision/directionless policies/Departments strayed from their primary objectives/Government not interested/serious/no political will	13	43.3
3. Corruption	7	23.3
4. Government lacks practical field knowledge/does not consult developers when making policies	6	20
5. Government does not want to be seen as supporting the developers/ Government does not trust developers	2	6.6
6. The government wants to establish itself as the largest developer/provider of affordable homes	1	3.3

The developers further complained that town planning does not match the growing population and that mechanisms such as high-density norms, re-densification measures, and land-pooling and land restructuring, if effectively used, could ease the shortage of land. They said that the lower densities permitted within the city limits constitute an inefficient use of land and can no longer be sustained.

Table 5.6 Developers' perceptions of what the government should do

Questions and answers	Number of developers who agreed (out of 30)
What should the government do to improve the supply of affordable homes?	
Introduce a single window for building approvals	12
Reform the Land Law	11
Reform the tax system	10
Improve town planning: Use new mapping technologies, employ qualified staff, update maps	7
Change their attitude towards developers	7
Reform building finance	5
Focus on infrastructure and access development	28

The 30 developers were asked what the government should be focusing on instead of building affordable homes, and 28 said infrastructure development; the other answers focussed on land, finance, taxes, and administrative reforms (Table 5.6).

Conclusion

Our discussions with these 30 developers show that they have different views as to the importance of these constraints on the supply of low-cost homes, but that they all limit the market in varying degrees. Many of them are related to one another, and to the supply constraints discussed in Chapter 7. For example, the availability of land is dependent on infrastructure development, and delays in approvals are related to bribes. All these constraints are part of the structure in which the market operates, and while some are more critical than others, they cannot be addressed in isolation.

Notes

1 In constraints where that is not the case, it has been duly mentioned.
2 At the time when the interview was recorded (2012), high rise was defined at 18 metres; a month later, it was changed to 30 metres or above.

6

WHY IS THE GOVERNMENT NOT DOING ANYTHING ABOUT IT?

The simple answer to this question is that the government is, in fact, doing a little, but change is not easy. If the Government of Chhattisgarh acknowledges its own lack of funds to house the urban poor, and is explicitly seeking private sector funding, why has this not been effective?

To explore this question, we interviewed 21 high-level officials who are associated with the provision of affordable housing in Chhattisgarh. We also conducted a focus group discussion with a group of senior state-level officials from State Bank of India (SBI). They included ministers, bureaucrats, and high-level government officials; bankers; heads of various government and non-government organisations; and local politicians who had some direct or indirect influence on the provision of low-cost housing in Chhattisgarh. They were chosen because of their involvement with the provision of such housing in Raipur, and were from the following four groups:

Group A – Housing and Environment Ministry
Group B – Ministry for Urban Development and the Department of Revenue
Group C – Banks and other financial institutions
Group D – Others, including the State Planning Commission, the State Finance Commission, two national universities, a charity that works on low-cost housing techniques, and the Chief Minister of the State

We picked out the highest-level officials from each group and approached them through formal letters to their offices, sometimes followed by a phone call. For the Chief Minister's interview, we were able to go through a personal contact who knew the Minister's chief of staff. All the interviews were conducted in their offices, and they lasted between 30 minutes and nearly 2 hours. All the interviews and group discussions were recorded and transcribed, and any comments which were made off the record have been indicated as such. The interviews were conducted in English and Hindi.

The aim of the interviews was to get the interviewees' perspectives on their own roles in the provision of low-cost homes in Chhattisgarh, their perspective on each of the demand and supply constraints which we had previously identified, and views of the possible emergence of a genuine market for low-cost housing in Chhattisgarh.

We also invited their opinions on the rationale for the roles of the current set of institutions, how easy or difficult it would be to change these institutions if need be; and who in their opinion would be capable of addressing the various issues. Finally, we asked their opinion on whether a genuine market for low-cost homes could arise if the institutional arrangements were different. They identified a number of institutional constraints to the evolution of such a market on both the supply and demand sides.

Rights

Insecure property rights affect the ability of poor people who live in the slums to secure credit for buying a house, due to their not having any proof of their address. Also, earlier experiences of being cheated in the real estate market lower their trust in real estate dealings, and their insecure employment makes house-hunting difficult.

Insecure rights increase transaction costs because of the time needed to verify that the property is free from dispute. The high transaction costs that face developers are also caused by the lengthy approval process, corruption, and high taxes, as well as the complex regulations that cause avoidable delays. As a result, the complex regulations reduce the enforcement capacity of the government. The combination of complexity and uncertainty of enforcement further feeds the cycle of insecure property rights that increase transaction costs.

Credit

The institutional arrangements make it difficult for a low-income household to get formal credit, and this is undoubtedly one of the biggest demand constraints, in addition to the low supply of low-cost housing. Informal credit for improving or repairing existing homes is more easily available, but this has major problems: It is only available in small amounts, so it cannot be used to buy a complete home in the formal market, and the person has to borrow from multiple sources to cover the cost of major repairs.

Informal credit from moneylenders is very expensive, and the annual interest can be as much as 60%, as discussed in Chapter 5. This makes long-term loans unaffordable.

Low-income people who live in slums do not have the documents they need to verify their identity, their address, or the source of their income, so are they are unable to obtain formal loans. The Unique Identification Authority of India (UIDAI) was established on 28 January 2009 and introduced a system known as Aadhar to give a number to all its citizens. This will in time overcome part of the identity problem, but it does not in itself provide proof of address. The difficulty of getting credit leads to ineffective demand from low-income households, which our respondents rated as the third most serious supply constraint.

The Reserve Bank of India (RBI) categorises housing as one of the six most important sectors and has mandated that 40% of banks' disbursals should be for mortgages. In spite of this, loans of under Rs. 500,000, or about 7000 USD, made up less than one-fourth of the total lending to the housing sector in 2010 (Cushman & Wakefield, 2014). Almost all of these loans are likely to have been for housing under government housing schemes for poorer people, because most people who earn below this amount, and are not formally employed, have no access to formal credit.

Sixteen of our 19 interviewees, including people from government and banks, said that the government should make it simpler to lend to poorer urban people, as it had for rural residents. Banks are allowed to make a loan to someone from a village on the basis of a letter from the head of the village council which certifies the borrower's identity and residence. The other three respondents believed the present rules should be retained in order to prevent bad loans.

Some poorer people can afford the deposit and monthly instalments, but because they cannot access formal credit, they have to borrow from the informal credit market; this promotes an informal land market. Because they cannot access formal credit and the land market itself is informal, their investments are inherently risky. The people who do this are fully aware that the transactions are not legal, so property claims cannot be upheld in a court of law, nor can disputes be settled legally. They do it because they need a place to live, because they see other people in the neighbourhood profiting from such deals, and in part because the brokers, or 'dalals', are good salesmen.

Trust in real estate dealings

Many poorer people, on the other hand, mistrust the formal real estate market. Several of our household respondents had heard rumours of people being cheated and losing their entire life savings in real estate transactions, and this discouraged them from becoming involved. They realised that stories about informal dealings did not necessarily apply to the formal market, but they did not have much faith in the formal system either. If a house was not delivered in the condition that was promised, for instance, they felt that they would not be able to defend their claims in a court. They did not feel that a certified document would always guarantee their investments. They did, however, have more confidence in houses built by government agencies, and would not be averse to buying them.

Developers often construct a model house, set a price for it, and then start taking bookings for homes of that design two or three years prior to actual construction. Because of delays in approvals, it may take many years for the homes to be completed. Even when planning permission has been granted for the entire project, building permission is given in stages. If a building has six floors, for instance, the layout is approved and fees are charged for all the floors, but actual permission to construct is only given for two or three floors. After they have been built, a fresh application has to be put in for permission to build the remaining floors.

Labour shortages and price increases also cause delays, so the developers are not able to keep to their promised prices. They may lower the quality, or increase the price, or both. While the private developers attributed such issues to a difficult business environment, 19 of our 21 interviewees tended to agree with the perspective of the low-income slum dwellers, and said that private developers are often dishonest. This made it necessary to have a lengthy approval process, as well as intermittent checks even after approval had been granted. It was difficult to find out whether these checks were actually carried out, or whether the government staff approved the projects because they had been bribed; none of the developers admitted that their work could be signed off without proper inspection. This distrust discourages slum dwellers from buying from private developers, and on the other hand, it increases the transaction costs because of the lengthy approval process.

House-hunting

Eighty three percent of our 211 slum household respondents said that searching for new homes was a problem. It takes time to verify that the ownership of a property is free of dispute, and that the property fulfils their needs and is affordable. Most of the slum dwellers whom we interviewed work in the informal sector, with no paid leave or job security; if they leave their work to search for housing, they lose income and may even lose their jobs. The insecurity of informal employment is an important cause of ill health; a study[1] in Mumbai found that around 85% of street vendors suffer from stress-related diseases such as migraine, hyperacidity (acid reflux), hypertension, and high blood pressure, largely because of their insecure working conditions.

The developers believed that it was difficult for people to look for homes because there is no formal market for low-cost housing. Most developers said that if the market was formalised, they would advertise and open booking offices in the slums in the evenings to service their clients, and would even organise transport for site viewings, so that potential clients would be aware of what was available and would be able to view it.

The government facilitators had varying opinions about house-hunting. Some said that low-income people who live in slums, like everyone else looking for a house, should make time in order to secure a home that meets their needs. Others said that it would not be too difficult for government agencies who build low-cost homes to run advertisements in slums or even run a bus service for potential buyers to view the houses, but that the high demand for low-cost housing means that there is no need for this. They did agree that the scarcity of low-cost homes meant that people had to spend more time looking for them.

Getting approval to build

We analysed the transaction costs of real estate development in terms of the time taken to get approvals for building construction. We estimated that the approval process, starting with the registration, would in total take between 18 and 26 months. Our informants agreed that developers who were politically connected, or had more money to spend on bribes, could get approvals in about 18 to 20 months, while it would take developers who did not have such resources between 24 and 26 months.

The developers clearly view these delays as a problem. Some[2] believe that corruption significantly exacerbates delays, while others[3] accept that corruption is a problem but consider that the delays are mainly caused largely by a combination of many issues, such as bureaucratic hurdles, resistance to change, red tape, unnecessary rules and regulations and departments, and most importantly, the government's inefficient and inadequate workforce.

The government facilitators whom we interviewed accepted that our estimates of the timeline were realistic, but they maintained that the procedures were necessary, and that delays were unavoidable, in order to check and control private businesses. As one informant said: "In spite of all these checks and balances, there are so many cases of illegal construction" (Interviewee-16F).

The interviews made it apparent that the government was aware of these problems and was working on an audit of the approval process, according to the 'simplifying transactions' recommendations of the Government of India's second Administrative Reforms Commission.[4] This Commission had recommended that transactions should be simplified, that a 'single window' approach should be adopted, that the levels of the bureaucracy should be reduced, and that time limits should be set for dealing with applications. The Commission also recommended that the existing departmental manuals and codes should be thoroughly reviewed and simplified, using precise terms, and that phrases such as 'left to the discretion of', 'as far as possible', or 'suitable decision may be taken' should be avoided in all rules and regulations governing the issue of permissions and licences. It also suggested the principle of 'positive silence': After the time limit, if a licence or permission has not been given, it should be deemed to have been granted.

Delay in approvals creates costs for the final buyer. This cost can be in terms of interest on loans taken for land purchase or construction, bribes and fees involved in actually getting the approval, or the hours and manpower involved in office visits and waiting time. Medium- and higher-income buyers may be able to afford these costs, but they can make low-cost housing unaffordable.

Buying the completed building

Corruption increases the transaction cost of buying and registering the sale of a house. One hundred sixty-five of our 211 low-income household respondents said that property registration was expensive, largely due to bribes. While most of them had never actually tried to register a property, their perception is not baseless. Studies on corruption and bribery faced by slum dwellers in India suggest that the problem is very serious (Paul & Shah, 1997; CMS Transparency, 2012; Hugi, 2012; Panchu & Rastogi, 2013). The CMS study (2012) found that three out of every four slum dwellers claimed they had been asked at least once in the previous 12 months to pay a bribe in order to receive food rations or free kerosene, or healthcare or municipal services such as public sanitation and waste removal. Over one-third said that they had been denied services at least once because they did not pay a bribe.

The building industry – taxation regulations

The Working Group on the Construction Sector (2011) concluded that high taxation of building inputs such as construction material, equipment, land, and services and taxes on work contracts, as well as the fact that construction is defined as an 'industry' as well as a 'service' for taxation purposes, were serious constraints to the supply of lowcost housing.

Voicing the industry's concern in 2016 at Natcon, the annual convention of the Confederation of Real Estate Developers Association of India (CREDAI), CREDAI national president Getamber Anand argued for clarity on the application of Goods and Services Tax (GST) on the industry. The developers pointed out that properties are immovable assets and not services. If GST is levied on the sector along with stamp duty and registration fee, it will push prices up by 18%, taking the overall tax to 23%. Our study reaches similar conclusions.

The World Bank's 'Doing Business in India' (2009) reports that property owners and developers resort to many different strategies to avoid property taxes, such as evading registration or using long-term leases, transfers under court decrees, and cooperative housing. Such practices, while legal, contribute further to the already muddled land administration system in India.

Credit for developers

The construction industry's lack of access to institutional finance is a major supply constraint. The Working Group on the Construction Sector for the Planning Commission for 2012–2017 reported that small contractors who lack a strong financial base execute over 90% of all construction work. Most of them use their own funds or borrow money from the informal market, at 30% annual interest or more, which leads to higher costs (2011).

The high interest rate and under-lending by banks are mutually rein-forcing. High interest rates deter developers from taking bank loans. This results in under-lending, as well as low repayments, which increase banks' operating costs. They cover this by setting even higher interest rates (see Figure 6.1), which leads to further under-lending. Also, banks with many non-performing loans attract more public scrutiny. This makes their loan officers more conservative, leading to further under-lending (Banerjee, Cole, & Duflo, 2003).

Banerjee et al. (2003) state that there is in India "definite evidence of very substantial under-lending with some firms clearly having the capacity to absorb much more capital at high rates of return". Less than 9% of all credit in India goes to construction, whereas the comparable figures for Japan, China, and Singapore were 15%, 14%, and 30%, respectively (Cushman & Wakefield, 2014). The high interest rates are related to under-lending. Because construction is not categorised as an 'industry', developers cannot have access to loans that banks are required to make to specific sectors. After the nationalisation of the banks,[5] lending to sectors such as agricul-ture, small-scale industries, and poorer people, which are collectively known as the Priority Sectors, was emphasised by the government. Sectoral targets are laid down by the government from time to time to encourage the sectors that are considered to need more investment to achieve balanced develop-ment. Construction firms are currently not categorised as an 'industry' by the Reserve Bank, which means that financial institutions that lend for hous-ing and urban development limit their lending to construction firms, and such loans are subject to high loan provisioning and security requirements.

There are many reasons why businesses of all kinds in India lack suf-ficient credit. Banerjee et al. (2003) found that bankers are often reluctant to change loan limits from year to year, irrespective of borrower-firms' prof-its. The loan officers are frightened of prosecution, as they can easily be charged with corruption if loans are not repaid; they are more concerned about avoiding bad loans and appearing corrupt than finding profitable lending opportunities. Bankers also prefer to make risk-free loans to the government, rather than screen and monitor private borrowers. Because they receive few rewards for making successful loans, bankers prefer simply to approve past loan limits rather than make new decisions.

The effect of government housing on the market

Government agencies do provide some subsidised housing to low-income people. This poses a risk for developers because there may not be enough demand for similar property at market prices. Our developer informants agreed that government provision depresses market prices and reduces the returns to private developers. The state and other interviewees, how-ever, believed that subsidised housing was a check on private sector greed,

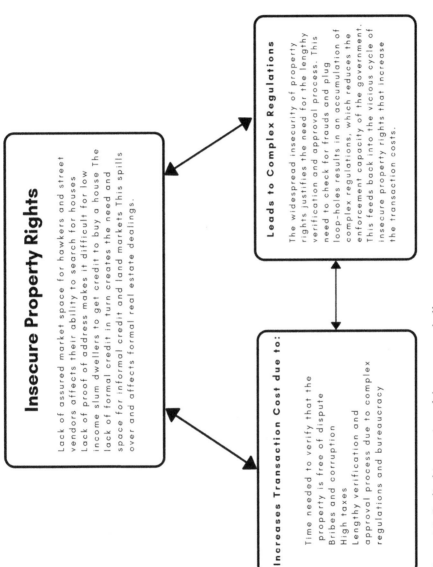

Insecure Property Rights

Lack of assured market space for hawkers and street vendors affects their ability to search for houses Lack of proof of address makes it difficult for low income slum dwellers to get credit to buy a house The lack of formal credit in turn creates the need and space for informal credit and land markets This spills over and affects formal real estate dealings.

Leads to Complex Regulations

The widespread insecurity of property rights justifies the need for the lengthy verification and approval process. This need to check for frauds and plug loop-holes results in an accumulation of complex regulations, which reduces the enforcement capacity of the government. This feeds back into the vicious cycle of insecure property rights that increase the transaction costs.

Increases Transaction Cost due to:

Time needed to verify that the property is free of dispute
Bribes and corruption
High taxes
Lengthy verification and approval process due to complex regulations and bureaucracy

Figure 6.1 Cyclical interaction of the causes and effects

although some felt that it could not be a powerful check, given that government provision serves only a fraction of the demand.

Some academic studies support this view. Sengupta and Tipple (2007) refute the assumption that public sector interventions restrict private housing. They are of the opinion that the housing need in poorer countries is so enormous that the private housing market is neither threatened nor undermined by investments in public housing. They argue that formal and informal private developers are and will remain the predominant actors in the housing market, and that the issue of 'control' over the market does not arise. Giving the example of Kolkata, they suggest that the city's 15 million people can only be housed by a large market, not by government regulations. There is enough potential for both private and public housing providers to operate in the market without threatening each other's business.

Restrictions on selling the dwellings

The regulations forbid developers who construct low-cost homes on the 15% of their land that is reserved for the purpose from selling them on the open market. Sales are further delayed by the process of allotment through the collector's office. The officials whom we met agreed that the checking system is not perfect, but they felt that some checks must be made when the housing stock is so low.

One official reported that developers were given permission to sell low-cost houses on the open market so long as the buyers gave an affidavit to certify their income levels. These houses had to satisfy certain minimum criteria; they had to be of at least 500 square feet in area and have basic amenities. The government assumed that the developers would follow the bare minimum requirements, and that no one other than slum dwellers would be interested in living in such small homes. The prices were not fixed by the government, and some developers instead built high-class studio apartments following the area requirements and sold them to students from wealthy families; the students could sign an affidavit to certify their low earnings.

Accumulation of regulations

Another official said that lawmakers are constantly trying to "plug the loopholes with small amendments", which results in the accumulation of regulations which are beyond the capacity of the government to enforce. This means that developers see the regulations as challenges to be surmounted rather than rules that need to be followed.

Zoning regulations – coloniser rule

In 1997, the state government introduced a new chapter on 'Colonisation' into the Chhattisgarh Municipal Corporation Act, 1956, wherein a land reservation for poorer people was introduced. In the original Act (1956), there was no specific provision for reservation of land for housing the urban poor.

> The developers would buy cheap land on the outskirts and give it to the government. Those lands would always be at places where there was no infrastructure, forget hospitals and schools, there would be no roads to get there, and the developer had done his part. So, a few years back, they introduced a shelter tax, that they could pay a lump-sum amount and if you pay that you won't have to leave 15% in your projects.
>
> (Interviewee-19B)

In 1998, the Chhattisgarh Nagar Palika[6] (Registration coloniser, Terms and Conditions) Rules were framed, which mandated the developers to reserve 15% of all developed land for poorer people in every residential colony in the urban area, and 25% of all developed land to which the Urban land (Ceiling and Regulation) Act, 1976, was applicable.

If a developer wished to sell newly constructed residential houses to poorer people instead of developed plots in his colony, then he had to build smaller houses on a quarter of the total area of the developed plot. However, these could not be sold in the open market but would be allotted by the government. If the developers of such colonies did not wish to develop plots or construct houses for economically weaker sections in their colonies, they would have to pay a compulsory 'shelter fee' – which, in an urban centre with a population above half a million (such as Raipur), was fixed at 100 rupees per square meter. This was to be used to provide basic services, such as sewage, drinking water, and public toilets, in slum areas.

> If your layout is within an acre then you don't have to reserve land for EWS. Then the colonisers started buying land from individual farmers, and got the layout passed in their [farmer's] name each of less than 1 acre, and then clubbed it together as one colony. And these kinds of colonies are the haphazardly developed colonies, because the layouts were passed individually, it is not easy to club them. There are many colonies here. . . . Go to Mahavir Nagar, Purena. It is a total hotchpotch. The whole area was never planned as such. If the shortest distance between point A and point B is 200 metres, you would need to travel 500 to 600 metres before you get there. The roads in such developments are all small and narrow – 20-foot roads. If they had gone in for a whole 10-acre planning their roads would need to be wider, but that never happened. Then the government realised that this won't work.
>
> (Interviewee-19B)

In order to discourage developers from choosing to pay the shelter fee rather than providing the necessary buildings themselves, some changes were introduced in 2004. The urban local body or the government agency acquiring the land had to pay the cost of the reserved 15% land to the builder, and the shelter fee was increased; for Raipur it amounted to Rs. 200 per square metre.

> That shelter tax is pretty heavy – Rs. 200/square metre, Rs. 20/ square foot on the total land. It is a huge amount and he has to pay it upfront for his layouts to be approved. And in spite of that, they prefer paying the shelter tax because they know that there is no way [that] they'll be able to sell even a single home if they club it with the EWS.
>
> (Interviewee-19B)

In 2005, another amendment was inserted: "Provided that such colonies which are to be developed by anybody under State Government for EWS (poorer people, or in the Indian phrase 'economically weaker sections') will be exempted from such conditions". The private sector was not building colonies for these people because of the existing institutional constraints and low profits, so in effect, this rule exempted the Housing Board and other government agencies from reserving such land.

The rule was still opposed, and our developers said that in 2011, after much lobbying by their association, some concessions were allowed. Developers of colonies had to allocate 15% of the land for poorer people, even for land on which the Urban Land (Ceiling and Regulation) Act, 1976 was applicable. In addition, they had to reserve at least 10% of the fully developed plots or offer constructed houses or flats of the prescribed size for poorer people. These homes could be sold by the developer in the open market. Developers were, however, still concerned about having to reserve land for poorer people in the same colony that was being built for the better-off people.

> I am talking from a social perspective. [I understand] Government has the obligation to house everybody. We do not want EWS housing in our compounds, but we need the facilitation [their services]. So let them have a separate compound, let them stay a furlong away and no one will have any issues, I am telling you. The idea that we should earmark spaces within each project [colony] is wrong. I understand their point, but I feel it should be a little apart, otherwise you are creating a nuisance and you are creating envy. If you space it well, they will be happier, and we will be happier.
>
> (Interviewee-04B)

We stopped getting layouts approved. Now they have realised that colonizers are reluctant [to build new colonies and get layouts approved] so they are in the process of removing the clause, I think. See on paper it all looks nice, that your maids and drivers will stay nearby, they come to work from there, but it doesn't work in our social matrix.

(Interviewee-19B)

During our fieldwork, the developers told us that their association was in consultation on this issue with the Department of Urban Development. They accepted that they might have to give up this land but were more concerned about the social issues that might arise if the land was reserved for poorer people within the colony compounds.

The 15% area for poorer people could now be "within a distance of not more than two kilometres from the municipal boundary provided that the land offered must be demarcated as 'residential' in the Master Plan, and it must have a clear and legal approach road". The total value of the land, as defined in the rule, must match the value of 15% of the land in the residential colony. Where the area of the proposed colony is one acre or more, in addition to transferring land for economically weaker sections,

the coloniser shall reserve at least ten percent of the fully developed plots or, in alternate offer, constructed houses/flats in the colony or in another location within a distance of not more than two kilometres from the boundary of the city, for persons belonging to the low income group.

In purely economic terms, the developers were still in the same position as before, but this amendment would make the reservation much more acceptable. Some of the government officials to whom we spoke said that some slum dwellers who are aware of the low level of official monitoring also try to exploit the system and to get more benefits from the government. The rules tend to be followed selectively, particularly when there is a high chance of getting caught, and the penalty is higher than the cost of following the regulation. For example, a developer might not dare to start a project without the necessary approvals even if it takes two years to get the approval, but once the project is approved, he may change the plans in the hope that the change will not be noticed.

Complicated accumulated regulations in an environment of insecure property rights and low overall enforcement increase transaction costs for both the developers and the government, and this further increases the costs of operating in the affordable housing market.

It is clear that these constraints on the market for low-cost housing are not isolated; they interact with one another. Figure 6.1 shows that the influence is multidirectional; this makes it difficult to establish the causes and effects, and thus to identify which constraints should be addressed first.

109

In order to identify ways in which the situation can be improved, it is vital to understand the relationship between the different institutional constraints. There are three separate types of housing provision – the market-based system for middle- and high-income buyers, the government-subsidised system for low-income people, and the informal system that operates in the slums, which is also market based.

Institutionalisation signifies some permanence to the structure, and thus some resistance to change. It is necessary to understand all the relevant institutions and how they interact, in order to understand the outcome. Any change must take account of their interactions. All the institutions that are involved must be examined, including the different interests they represent and how they all influence each other and the outcome. Our work draws on Michael Ball's (1983) 'structure of housing provision' framework to analyse the effect of institutions on housing markets, and is based on the assumption that there is a coherent structure of institutions to regulate housing provision.

We have identified several institutional constraints to the demand for and supply of affordable housing in Raipur, and some of these are mentioned in industry and government reports on low-cost housing in India. These constraints cannot be addressed in isolation, as they are not independent of each other. Credit is a demand constraint; however, it leads to a supply constraint of ineffective demand. Similarly, public provision of housing lowers the market price of such housing. Slum upgrading and slum clearance programmes both affect the demand. And the national employment generation scheme for rural areas is said to have resulted in a shortage of casual labour for building in urban centres. Lack of access to credit for low-income households in slums, who could afford to pay for housing, leads to a vibrant informal land market. And cheating in informal land markets can lead to low confidence in the real estate sector in general.

These constraints are often the result of complex institutional arrangements, so that solutions which might work in a different institutional context might not work in Raipur or in India generally. For example, the credit problem cannot be resolved merely by setting up institutions that supply loans at low interest rates. Our survey in Raipur, where the suggested monthly mortgage instalments were based on the market rate of 12%, showed that many households could afford to buy at that interest rate. They did not need interest subsidies, but they were unable to get loans because they did not have proof of identity and address.

The constraints to the low-cost housing market are not merely related to each other; they are connected to the whole of society and the economy. Lower taxes would facilitate the market, but they would also reduce government's revenues. Changes can only be made after a comprehensive socio-economic cost–benefit analysis.

A poor household can obtain housing through informal or formal means. If we analyse this using the additional information gathered by the surveys, we can see that there are two systems operating in Raipur.

Informal systems in the slums

A typical immigrant into Raipur who is looking for work usually comes alone from his rural village. Sometimes, his oldest son of perhaps 15 to 16 years may come with him. He will live in a shared room with a stove in the corner and some pots and pans for cooking and a few food storage containers. He will usually find work in one of the factories on the outskirts of the city and will live in one of the nearby slum villages such as Gondwara, which was one of the areas where we carried out our research. Such people usually send money to their families who still live in their rural village. Some are seasonal migrants, but most recent immigrants into the city whom we surveyed had not gone back home in over a year or even two or three years. Most of the older migrants said that if they still have a job after about five years, they bring their families to the city and look for more permanent accommodation.

Depending on the location and land prices in the informal market, they buy, rent, or sometimes merely occupy the land as squatters, but they said that because of the increasing numbers of migrants, new immigrants can no longer find free land for squatting. "The old-timers", as they called themselves, told us that when they came into the city 20 or 30 years ago, they occupied public land free of cost by filling up the low-lying marshy ponds. This was hard work and they could only do it after their day jobs, and most of them feel entitled to the land that they "created". Newcomers, who had migrated in the last 10 years or so, usually had to buy or rent their houses.

The older houses were built with temporary materials and were often rebuilt and expanded to suit the needs of a growing family. Extensions are reportedly easily rentable and are always in demand, as is most other housing and land. Monthly rents vary from Rs. 800–1200 (11–16 USD), while depending on size and location, houses are sold for anywhere between Rs. 50,000 to Rs. 12 lacs (700 USD – 16,000 USD).

Informal land brokers assist the poor who live in the slums to buy and sell property. It is bought largely with cash but also with the help of informal credit. Figure 6.2 illustrates the system whereby informal housing is acquired. One striking aspect of this is how closely it mirrors a typical formal market system, as the process of exchange is fundamentally the same. Another striking aspect of the system is that it works without any formal contracts or enforcement and dispute redressal mechanisms.

The usual informal enforcement mechanism is to put pressure on the person concerned. There was no mention of violence or violent threats, and if

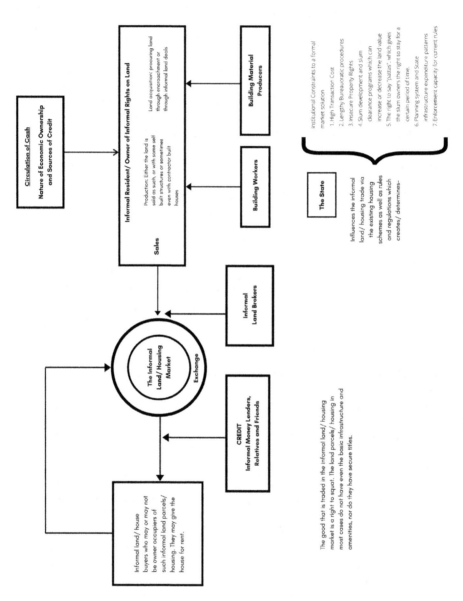

Figure 6.2 Current structure of housing provision for informal low-cost housing in Raipur

there was a need for redress it was usually done by changing the time or amount of money or providing a different piece of land.

The asset that is traded in the informal market is unsecured access to land or a house or, in other words, a 'right to squat'. The land and houses lack basic infrastructure and amenities, and buyers do not acquire legally enforceable titles. Their titles are honoured by the community, but not by the government. If the government clears the slum, or builds a new project on the land, the slum dwellers may or may not be compensated. The government is not legally obliged to compensate slum dwellers for taking 'their' land, although they may do so as a political favour. The buyers, therefore, have no insurance or security for their investment. Government slum upgrading programmes do provide selective basic infrastructure in some areas, and land in these areas costs more than in areas without any amenities. The households do not get legal titles, nor are the areas considered to be 'formal', even after the slums have been upgraded.

The government low-cost housing system

The official system for the supply of low-cost housing in Raipur has remained essentially the same since 2004 in spite of changing policies. It provides houses with basic amenities and legal titles and works mainly through three agencies – the Chhattisgarh Housing Board (or CGHB), the Raipur Development Authority (RDA), and the Raipur Municipal Corporation (RMC). Each of these is headed by a political appointee and managed by a senior bureaucrat. They are in charge of the housing projects undertaken by their respective agencies, which includes acquiring land, managing the design and construction bids, and allotting of houses to homeowners. The three agencies sometimes also guarantee the loans taken out by the homeowners.

While the processes are more or less similar, each project has its own guidelines for implementation. These agencies apply to the District Collector for land. If it is public land, the Collector can allot it directly. If it is private land, the Collector has to purchase it and then allot it to the agency. The three agencies have each accumulated a stock of land so that they do not have to acquire new property each time they need it. The RMC also administers the land that is acquired from private developers as part of the area, which is reserved for low-income people, and is the only one of the three agencies that is building low-cost homes. Currently, only the RMC is building on this land. Additional land can also be allotted directly by the state government for certain projects.

Once the land is secured, the agencies call for a bid from architects to provide design and technical specifications for the project. The winning bid is selected by the agency, which then invites a second bid for construction of the selected design. Sometimes both bids are combined, and the RMC awards the design and construction to one party in a single process. Private architects and construction firms are the usual bidders for these contracts, but some of them are bid, won, and executed by a local NGO. Private contractors usually work on a fixed 10% profit margin. They sometimes employ subcontractors but more often do the work themselves, working with building workers and material producers. Some projects in Chhattisgarh were built exclusively for low-income people, but in most cases the housing is mixed in government projects; the high-income housing is built to cross-subsidise the costs of providing housing for lower-income people.

The organisations that construct the houses can borrow central or state funds to finance the projects, depending on the housing scheme. Mortgages are provided by banks or by the Housing and Urban Development Organisation and other similar organisations. Government agencies sometimes act as third-party guarantors. Mortgages are only available to low-income families who have the necessary documents, which effectively limits such houses to low-income households with a member who is employed by the government.

The Chhattisgarh Government Housing Board holds *Awas Melas*, or Housing Fairs, to enable the various government agencies to provide information about their housing schemes, details of the Board's properties which are available for allotment and sale, and a place where interested low-income households can submit application forms. People can also visit the agencies' offices or obtain the information from their websites. These fairs also serve as political propaganda to show how the state government is working towards its goal of 'housing for all'.

The government agencies that build subsidised housing invite applications for the new housing. These applications are then verified, and the houses are allotted by lottery because the number of applications exceeds the number of homes. The houses are usually allotted in the name of a female member or held jointly. The new owners are not allowed to sell the houses for 10 years.

Once all the houses have been sold, the common property on which they stand is transferred to the local authorities for routine maintenance, which is funded by a property tax. These services include waste disposal, maintenance of approach roads, drainage, water supply, and electricity.

For regular maintenance of the housing colony, the owners are encouraged to form a society that will be in charge of maintenance and upkeep of the buildings. The local authority supports the formation of such societies.

The initiation and completion of housing projects are major political events, widely publicised and chaired by either the Chief Minister or Housing Minister of the State. The project starts with the ceremonial laying of the foundation stone and *bhoomi pujan* or groundbreaking prayers. Once the project is completed, the houses are handed over to the government agency, which then holds an inauguration ceremony to hand over the keys and documents to the allotted homeowners.

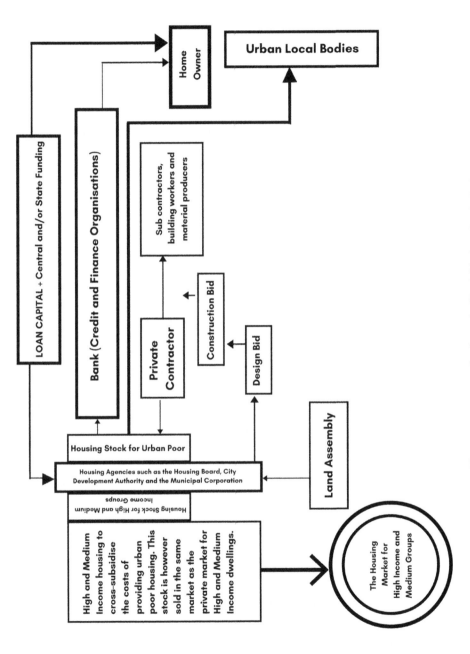

Figure 6.3 Current structure of housing provision for formal affordable housing in Raipur

It is clear that the many constraints to low-cost housing development are interrelated and the institutions are interconnected through repeated exchanges, so that the formal and informal systems have become institutionalised into two separate but linked structures that produce a predictable set of behaviours. Because the institutions are connected to each other in complex ways, they cannot be isolated from one another.

Housing policy

The following section outlines the changes in housing policy in Chhattisgarh that took place between the 1950s and 2020, and their results or the lack thereof. These changes and their consequences show that although the need for change was recognised, the changes that were made did not remedy the problems. We then argue that institutional inertia prevented this change.

Need for change recognised but the situation is not changing

Changes in housing policy, and the results

Indian national housing policy has evolved over the years. In the early 1950s, housing was seen as a service which most people should provide for themselves. By the late 1950s it came to be regarded as part of social welfare, and by the late 1980s and into the early 1990s it came to be recognised as a social and economic prerequisite for growth (Planning Commission, 1992). Although the policies for low-cost housing changed, the government remained the largest formal provider.

When housing policy as stated in planning and other documents is compared with the aims and objectives of the government departments and subsidiary organisations set up for housing provision, it is clear that the change in housing policy from public provision to private financing and market provision has largely remained an unfulfilled aspiration. This is partly because the policies were declarations of intent with no legal basis, and in part because they were not developed into implementable schemes with adequate resources, such as budget allocations or capacity building and restructuring of facilitating organisations.

There were also changes in policy at the state level. When the new State of Chhattisgarh was formed in 2000, the state government had a chance to break away from the subsidy culture and to open up housing to the private sector. This is precisely what it did. The Housing Board was disbanded, and housing was privatised. Private sector housing provision did increase, but it was confined to the upper end of the market.

Raipur was a new state capital with new employment opportunities, and this increased migration into the city. The formal low-cost housing market was not served, the informal housing market became active, and the number of slums increased. The slum population grew by over 60% between 1991 and 2001, and by 2005 it had reached about 350,000, which was an increase of 53% since 1991 (GTZ ASEM, 2010). When a new political party came to power in 2004, they claimed that the experiments of the previous government had failed, and they reestablished the Housing Board. The new government portrayed itself as the provider for the poor; this point was reflected in the interviews we had with a minister and a senior bureaucrat who wanted to show that the government was determined to fulfil the housing needs of the poor, irrespective of private sector participation.

The schemes they introduced provided subsidised housing but were limited by the available resources. Half of the 21 facilitators whom we interviewed, when asked, as to what was their role in promoting affordable housing, saw themselves as developers whose role was to 'plan and execute new housing developments'. This did not bode well for the development of a formal market in low-income housing. The Raipur Development Authority (RDA) is in charge of developing new infrastructure for the city, but ever since its formation it has mainly worked on housing development projects. The newly formed state government decided to create a planned new city for Raipur, which was to be called *Naya Raipur* or New Raipur. For this purpose, a special greenfield area was notified under section 64 of the Town and Country Planning Act. The Naya Raipur Development Authority (NRDA) was formed to serve as the nodal agency undertaking comprehensive development of the city, but there was no organisation to provide new infrastructure for the city, or to create the enabling strategy which the state's housing policy has claimed to support since 1988. While all the facilitators agreed that the lack of affordable housing was a problem, none of them saw themselves or any other institution as being responsible for creating a market for low-cost housing.

The state departments and government agencies in the housing sector have never been properly re-organised to carry out their changing objectives; they have continued to work in the same way. The departmental roles in the provision of low-cost housing are determined according to specified targets and tend to be perceived in narrow terms, such as providing credit for a certain number of low-income families under various government projects, procuring land under certain schemes, or fulfilling certain building targets.

Even for policy formulation, tasks are narrowly defined, such as drafting the policy or designing a scheme in accordance with the budget. While the policy serves as a declaration of intent, there is no organisation in charge of actually implementing it. Each housing scheme has its own parameters or regulations for project execution. These regulations tend to be independent of the overall policy. Some policy objectives, such as zoning laws for low-cost housing, are written into the Town and Country Planning Act or Municipal Act and are therefore legally enforceable. Others such as "seeking private sector participation" or "facilitating the creation of a market" remain ambiguous.

Centre–state relationships

Housing policy and schemes do not appear to relate to each other at the state or the national level. This lack of connection between national housing policy that aims to enable the private sector, and housing schemes that continue with government provision of subsidised housing, is partly a result of relations between central and state governments. At the centre, the Ministry for Housing and Urban Poverty Alleviation drafts national housing policy. The centre's programmes, which are intended to give effect to national policy, are channelled to the state governments through the State Urban Development Authority (SUDA) – which, in Chhattisgarh, carries out slum upgrading programmes. The state housing policy is drafted by the state government, and the Housing Board is in charge of the state housing schemes.

While the professed aim of Indian housing policy is to enable housing development, as discussed in Chapter 2, the only housing scheme introduced by the central government that comes even close to having a set of guidelines promoting the participation of the private sector is the *Affordable Housing in Partnership* document (MoHUPA, 2009). But even that assumes that the private sector will be interested in building homes for the poor and does not consider the existing institutional constraints that limit the evolution of a market. The Affordable Housing in Partnership scheme was subsumed by the Pradhan Mantri Awas Yojna, which was introduced in 2014.

As critics[7] of Indian housing policy point out, one glaring issue is the disparity between aims and strategies on the one hand, and the available financial resources and managerial capacity on the other. The guidelines are unrealistic and generalised and are only meant to be recommendations on the basis of which state governments should design their own schemes, given that the regulation of land and housing fall in the domain of the state. For these enabling guidelines to be effective, they must at least identify and address the demand and supply constraints, so that they can be translated into schemes in which the private sector is interested to participate.

The provision of low-cost housing is only one of the many tasks for which both the state and central government have generated schemes in order to provide housing, and there are also several small schemes run by various state government agencies with centre or state funds, where the agency acts as a housing developer and develops a housing colony under the particular scheme. Each state also receives central government funding for housing and urban development through various central government schemes, such as the slum upgrading programme known as the Rajiv Awas Yojana.

The governance structures that are suitable for a programme that seeks long-term systemic change, such as a market-enabling strategy, are different from those that are needed to respond to more short-term goals, such as building houses. This difference does not seem to have been considered. The result is that the official departments – which are, in any case, understaffed – are kept busy with the more immediate targets and deadlines of the short-term schemes, which have clear guidelines and deliverables.

Inertia in land and infrastructure supply

The town and country planning unit in Chhattisgarh is in some sense a colonial inheritance, in that Indian urban master plans still draw their inspiration from the Delhi Master Plan prepared under the Delhi Development Act of 1957, which was itself based on the 1947 British Town and Country Planning Act. The present urban development planning system caters only to the requirements of the Act, whereby almost every city has the same general objectives. The objectives of the plan are generally not related to the availability of finance, so that most proposals are not executed because of lack of funds, or because they are not aligned with the priorities of the government. Also, there is no regular monitoring, evaluation, or management of these plans, so that planning is no more than unfulfilled constitutional obligation (Kumar & Pandit, 2013).

A similar opinion was reflected in a presentation made by the Raipur Development Authority in 2013 for a National Workshop on Land Pooling for Real Estate Development in New Delhi:

> In the past, there has been an absence of [integrated] planning [for the city] as a whole . . . planning [in] parts has led to a haphazard development with a lack of proper infrastructure. The result has been development of slums and unorganised/unapproved constructions.

City master plans in theory define land uses for the next 10 years. A developer cannot buy cheap agricultural land and expect to be able to change the land use. However, without implementation capacity, officials are unable to prevent slums from mushrooming in areas that are reserved for other purposes. This has reduced the process of master planning into a regularising exercise, where the plan is readjusted every 10 years to reflect the ground reality. The slums are regularised, and the initial planned land use for the area is changed to reflect the actual pattern on the ground.

The developers to whom we spoke criticised the past and current master plans of Raipur; they said they were not in keeping with the available resources and the enforcement capacities of the city, nor with the unprecedented population growth and migration. Table 6.1 shows the range of official floor space indices (FSI) in some Indian cities and some cities in other countries. In Raipur, the highest FSI at the time of our fieldwork was 1.25, and it was 2 in the city centre. These FSI, which are good measures of density for India, are well below those in other major cities, many of which are in countries with much lower population density.

Table 6.1 Floor space indices in India and elsewhere

Floor space indices in some Indian cities and other countries

City	Area	Maximum FSI/FAR
Kolkata	Town centre	3.00
Bengaluru (near metro stations)	Town centre	4.00
Mumbai	Island City	1.33
	Suburbs	2.70
Delhi	Town centre	3.50
Chennai	City	3.50
Country	**City**	**Maximum FSI/FAR**
Bahrain	Bahrain	17
USA	New York City downtown	15
USA	Los Angeles downtown	13
USA	Chicago downtown	12
China	Hong Kong	12
USA	San Francisco	9
Thailand	Bangkok	8

Source: Cushman and Wakefield Research

Most of the developers whom we interviewed said that one of the side effects of the lack of sound planning is the shortage of land for formal housing development. The *Approach to the 12th Five-Year Plan* document (The Planning Commission, 2011) recognises that, in many ways, the regulations that are intended to manage densities and discourage migration, limit the supply of land and require formal sector housing to consume more land than the developers would otherwise chose. These regulations include low density measures, high standards for parking, high land surface coverage limits, wide setbacks from roads, and wide roads. The document states that these outdated planning regulations are one of the causes of urban sprawl, and that they generally push up the price of land and the cost of service delivery.

Another cause of the shortage of land for development is the lack of infrastructure and transport routes to the outskirts of cities. The development of trunk roads and social infrastructure is largely the responsibility of state governments. Most of our informants agreed that the Raipur Development Authority, which was set up to implement the master plan, has not been very successful, although they differed as to why this was so. Some developers said that because the RDA is a government agency headed by an elected representative, it therefore pursues 'quick wins' such as housing projects, rather than dealing with slow and undramatic infrastructure development projects.

The RDA staff say that their failure to implement the master plan is due to lacking sufficient funds. The McKinsey Global Institute for 2010 states that India's annual capital spending on urban infrastructure of 17 USD per head is only 14% of China's 116 USD and 4% of the United Kingdom's 391 USD,[8] and that India would have to invest 1.2 trillion USD in its cities over the next 20 years to catch up. This is equivalent to 134 USD per head per year, and it would represent an increase in urban infrastructure spending from 0.5% of GDP to 2%. Kumar and Pandit (2013) agree; they argue that state budgets, as well as the market price of land, should be used as a tool for guiding land use in master plans. Some of those whom we interviewed, however, while not wanting to defend the RDA, argued that master plans are easier to draft and implement in undeveloped areas such as Naya Raipur, the new capital area, than in existing unplanned cities such as Raipur.

It is important to note that municipalities and development authorities have been deliberately starved of state and centre funds, to encourage them to raise funds from the market through bonds and user fees and to borrow from international financial institutions. Nevertheless, to date it remains very difficult for municipalities, which have low credit ratings and other problems, to do this.

Municipalities are short of funds and staff, and the guidelines for drafting and implementing master plans, which determine how cities make and enforce land and space choices, are not consistent with demographic needs. The Central Government's Ministry of Urban Development is responsible for revising the guidelines for drafting and implementing urban development plans, but little has changed.[9] The Chhattisgarh state government has also made some amendments, such as introducing land reservation for low-cost housing, but such piecemeal amendments also increase the number of regulations, which in turn increases the transaction costs.

Institutional inertia prevents housing policy from changing

The low-cost housing problem is not adequately dealt with, largely because of institutional inertia; various factors prevent institutions from changing, even when it has been decided that change is needed. We believe that 'clientelism' is one of the main reasons for institutional inertia in Raipur.

It can be argued that there are two forms of clientelism (Hopkin, 2006), the old and the political. In feudal society, the patron provided clients with the basic means of subsistence and clients reciprocated with a combination of economic goods and services such as rent, labour, and part of their crops, and social acts of deference and loyalty. The new form of *political clientelism* involves political parties with bureaucratised structures, which have replaced the feudal lords as patrons.

The main difference between the two forms is that in the old system, the client voted automatically for the patron out of deference and the promise of protection and aid, whereas the newer type of client shops around for the patron who offers the best deal, and may even switch patrons if the flow of benefits dries up. The new clientelism, in this way, resembles a market exchange in which clients seek to maximise utility irrespective of any sense of obligation.

Other authorities[10] present the different perspective of a broker-mediated model, wherein the broker is considered a field operative of the political parties who closely knows his client base in terms of their needs and preferences, both political and otherwise. He is in charge of the distribution of favours and of ensuring that the voters cast their votes for the party concerned. However, the broker has his own interests, which are not always aligned with those of the party, and hence he is an imperfect agent who imposes his own costs on the political parties and can threaten to withdraw his vote base if his needs are not met. This model closely resembles the clientelist pattern in Raipur.

Clientelism can therefore be understood as a method of getting votes, as an exchange of goods and services for political support (Stokes, Dunning, Nazareno, & Brusco, 2013). This clientelist form of democracy is a useful way of understanding the role of a minister or elected representative in India, where political support is sought in exchange for goods and services; hence, subsidies play a major role in governance in India. Subsidies are widely publicised, and this helps political parties to establish their brand and their authority over their brokers in the distributive game.

It has been argued (Bardhan, 1984; Baken, 2003) that the socialist ideology of the founders of independent India allowed disproportionate spending in subsidies, and thus distorted the management and use of capital in the public sector. Under such a system, politicians have an incentive to choose policies based on their short-term political appeal, such as subsidies that are identified with a political party, rather than policies which are based on growth or poverty reduction strategies, such as universal access to basic services. These short-term policies make it difficult to reduce inequality, and the lack of political commitment to equity tends to preserve the status quo (Fritz, Katayama, & Simle, 2008).

Subsidies also contribute considerably to family incomes in the slums. Affordable housing is the most politically popular type of subsidy (Baken, 2003), but it is not the only one. Under one scheme, 100,000 tablet computers were given to poor children, many of whom lived in villages that were not internet connected or wi-fi enabled, and the equivalent of almost 6 million USD was allocated to give bicycles to schoolchildren. Under the food subsidy programme, for example, 35 kilograms of rice is given to each low-income family at a price of Rs. 2 per kilogram, compared with the market price, which usually varies between Rs. 25–40 per kilogram. In addition to the food subsidy, the Rajiv Swasthya Bima Yojana (RSBY) provides health insurance up to Rs. 35,000 per annum per family. The food subsidy scheme is worth some Rs. 10,000 per year, and all together, a typical poor family receives subsidies worth some Rs. 50,000, or almost 700 USD per annum. The targeting of these subsidies and their actual availability have often been questioned. This point was considered during our fieldwork; about 8% of the low-income families who said that they could afford to pay for a house, would not be able to do so if they faced a medical emergency or if food subsidies were withdrawn.

Another subsidy programme that indirectly affects the housing market is the rural employment generation (MG-NREGA) scheme, which our developer respondents mentioned as a cause of building labour shortage. This guarantees 100 days of work to rural labour in their villages, at wages which are sometimes higher than the market wage rate. The continuation of such subsidy schemes is another barrier to the emergence of a genuine market for low-cost housing.

Clientelism also affects the way political decisions are made. There is no room for wider debates on long-term issues. Politicians win elections on the basis of promises of subsidies and so on, and while they are in office, most of their energy is spent delivering on those promises in order to be re-elected. The promises they make are not about systemic changes but instead concern the urgent needs of individual slum dwellers.

While waiting for two hours in the office of the Mayor of Raipur for an interview which never happened, there was an opportunity to observe this process. People asked for a hand pump in their neighbourhood, for a road to be fixed, for the cancellation of a slum clearance order, for a junior government employee to be transferred to be with his family, for somebody's son to be given a job in place of his father who had lost his life on the job; these were some of the varied petitions that were presented.

A minister's budget can be spent as he decides, and it is understood that it will be used in a way that will get him re-elected. For example, the Chhattisgarh State Ministry of Urban Development and Housing, which has a large budget, was split into two – the Ministry of Urban Development and the Ministry of Housing – apparently in order to split the budget between two people, rather than having it concentrated with one minister who might be seen as more 'generous' because he provided more subsidies.

Politicians appear to believe that they should be able to interfere in the implementation of programmes on behalf of their electorate (Baken, 2003). One official whom we interviewed complained that this patronage behaviour and favouritism complicated his job because of the time and energy he had to spend on "resist[ing] . . . politicians who are very dominating . . . while implement[ing] government policies" (Interviewee-04F).

City-level politicians are more involved in implementing policies than in formulating them. Two of those whom we interviewed said that it would be risky to make the radical changes which would be needed to create a genuine market in low-cost housing because it would cause a shock to the system and might alienate the electorate.

This expectation is supported by the behaviour of the slum dwellers who have come to expect such benefits from the government; this view is freely acknowledged by most slum households and shared by developers, bureaucrats, and politicians alike. When they were asked whom they considered as their ally if they were threatened with eviction, 31% of the households mentioned their local political councillor or *Parshad*, who they believed would either get them compensation or a free home.

Loan defaults are another adverse outcome of this clientelist approach. Government-subsidised houses are considered as handouts by most recipients. Based on their earlier experiences[11] with government loans, slum dwellers sign an already heavily subsidised contract agreement in the expectation that their payment will be reduced or waived with the help of their councillors. In Raipur, this meant that many RDA projects (Interviewees -06F & -20F) were unable to recover their costs; the slum dwellers were advised by their local politicians to default on their loans, although they were able to repay.

Many slum dwellers said that their power to vote was their only strength, which they have learned to wield to their benefit. If a councillor does not agree to their demands, they approach the opposition candidate, who may then win the election on the promise of meeting their demands. In a clientelist system, democratic representation means that poor people often lack the education and information they would need to be able to monitor the activities of their elected representatives. They are therefore unlikely to value abstract promises. Unless they receive concrete, tangible benefits, they are unlikely to reward representatives who say they are working on a particular policy, even if the claim is true (Taylor-Robinson, 2010).

Many developers complained that slum dwellers enjoyed political favours. They felt that they were expected to adhere strictly to planning and building codes (Interviewee-19B), while informal developers in the slums were allowed to build houses without having to follow any guidelines (Interviewee-22B). The bureaucrats and politicians acknowledged that slum dwellers have some influence as part of their mutual relationship. The slum dwellers often manage to get a *patta* or 'right to stay' for a certain period of time through the elected representatives or a minister, and then at the end of the given time period, having built a community in the slum, they resist relocation.

The "permissive implementation of master plans" mentioned previously is, according to Baken (2003), an implicit government policy that considers squatting to be a viable way of solving the problem of land delivery to the poor, "on the principle of allowing squatting to emerge and cleaning them up [with slum redevelopment schemes] whenever the occasion arises". Mahadevia et al. (2009) consider such land as space that the occupants have gained through the political process of 'patron–client' relationship and therefore rightfully consider as belonging to them.

The politicians whom we interviewed considered that it would be risky to create a formal market for low-cost housing because it would involve a complicated change with no assurance that it would be successful. Giving the example of the Indramma Yojana, a housing scheme in neighbouring Telangana state, the Minister explained that local housing projects are more likely to succeed than any attempt to create a genuine market.

He explained that these are independent small-scale schemes over which the Minister has considerable control, or schemes that are seen more as the projects of the authority concerned rather than being part of statewide policies (Interviewee-20F). Most government agencies are headed by an elected representative for whom long-term goals are risky because they need the continued support of the next government. A short-term housing project has a better chance of successful completion than a long-term infrastructure development project that will need some time to take off because of the land acquisition. It will cause major inconvenience in terms of traffic disruption, dust, and pollution in the initial years, and may even be scrapped by the initial sponsor's successor. Also, if the politician who initiates the project is not re-elected but the project continues, the initiating politician will not get any credit for the successfully finished project. The focus is therefore on projects which can be completed within three to five years, so that politicians can take credit for them.

The clientelist form of democracy thus leads to short-term decision making, because people expect rapid tangible rewards in exchange for their political support. This reinforces the informal approach to low-cost housing provision and is one of the reasons why there has been no real move towards the new policy of creating a market for such housing. In effect, clientelism serves as an alternative to the market.

Implications for changing housing policy

It is clear that the deregulation and privatisation which were recommended by the World Bank (1993) and adopted by both the national and the state governments, do not automatically lead to the formation of a market, especially in the complex conditions of Raipur. A formal market will not emerge if new policies are merely laid on top of the existing structure. Such a market will only emerge if the institutional constraints are addressed and the whole structure of housing provision is restructured. Markets will only emerge when the barriers are removed and if there is a genuine potential for them. Removing barriers will not necessarily result in a market, and any new market will have to have its own new rules and regulations. This will be discussed further in Chapter 7.

However important it may seem to be to introduce change, people are slow to change their ways of thinking and acting. Nine of the 19 authoritative people to whom we spoke believed that a fundamental change would need a change in attitudes amongst everyone concerned – the low-income people who live in slums, the developers, and the government officials. This, they said, would not be easy.

One potentially important improvement, the results of which illustrate the difficulty of changing behaviours, is the Real Estate Regulation and Development Act, popularly known as RERA, which the Government of India introduced in May 2016. The act was introduced to increase transparency in real estate dealings, and thereby protect homebuyers and encourage investments. The provisions of the act were to be enforced from May 2017. This gave developers time to prepare for the new requirements.

The act requires all real estate agents or 'brokers' to register with the RERA before facilitating the sale or purchase of any property. They are also mandated to put up all the documents related to the project approvals and land title deed records, and to list the project details and timelines. To some extent, the act corrects for the unequal bargaining power by giving buyers the right to seek compensation and withdraw their entire investment along with interest, in case the builder misrepresents the facts in advertisements. The developers have to quote prices based on 'carpet area' – that is, the useable space within the dwelling – not on the whole built-up area, which includes common areas such as elevators and corridors.

A developer is not allowed to receive more than 10% of the cost of the dwelling, without first entering into a registered agreement for sale. There is also a strict legal obligation to develop the project in accordance with the sanctioned layout plans and specifications as approved by the competent authorities. The Act also prohibits money that might have come from untaxed sources being used in the development of projects; 70% of the money has to be deposited in bank accounts through cheques.

A well-regulated and monitored real estate market is likely to increase the general level of trust in formal real estate dealings and may help increase investments in the sector. Not many studies have been made about the effects of RERA on the market, but a survey of home buyers in Chennai indicated that even some years after the act had come into effect, homebuyers were still unaware of many aspects of real estate transaction. The survey also found that it has not yet become normal practice for buyers to check, verify, and validate homes that they intend to purchase (Vasumathi, 2018). It takes time for new institutional arrangements such as RERA to build trust in the general population.

Initiatives such as RERA that attempt to improve the regulatory system may in time make some improvement at the margins, but they are unlikely to effect the massive change which is needed to make a significant impact on India's, and thus the world's, most appalling housing situation. At around the same time, the Government of India introduced a massive new programme, known as the PMAY, which builds on earlier efforts to solve the problem through even greater levels of subsidy. This has achieved some results, at enormous expense, but it is not clear whether or not it will eventually exacerbate the problem by continually increasing people's dependence on subsidy.

The Pradhan Mantri Awas Yojana (PMAY) programme, also known as the "housing for all" programme, was launched on 25 June 2015 with the stated objective of providing dwellings to all eligible beneficiaries by 2022. The total demand and target for the programme was estimated to amount to 11.2 million dwellings.

The dwellings can be provided in one of four ways depending on applicants' incomes, their financial resources, and the availability of land. In existing slum areas which have been chosen for redevelopment, a grant of Rs. 100,000 (or about 1300 USD) is given to each householder. Secondly, urban poor and middle-income households who apply for housing loans from authorised institutions are eligible for the credit linked subsidy scheme, under which they can get an interest subsidy of between 3% and 6.5% on loans of between Rs. 600,000 and Rs. 1,200,000 (between 8000 and 16,000 USD), up to an upper limit of almost Rs. 300,000 (or about 4000 USD) per dwelling. The third approach is an amendment to an earlier scheme whereby the central government gives a subsidy of Rs. 150,000 (or about 2000 USD) per dwelling to private developers on the condition that the houses are allotted to very poor households, and that 35% of the houses in a given housing development project must be reserved for the very poor.

Under the fourth method, the Central Government gives very poor households grants of Rs. 150,000 (or about 2000 USD) on the condition that they can provide documents to prove their income levels; this can be used either to construct new houses or to improve existing houses, and the total living area must not be more than 30 square meters.

Under this last scheme, none of the members of the household are allowed to own a permanent house anywhere in India, and their current slum dwelling must be below 21 square metres. Preference is given to waste pickers; to women, and particularly to widows; and to people who belong to one of the many special groups in India who are eligible for such things, including the lower castes and tribal people, certain other so-called 'backward' classes and minorities, and disabled and transgender people who are also very poor.

The PMAY scheme used revised definitions for very poor, poor, and middle-income households. Very poor households are those with an annual income of up to Rs. 300,000; poor households are defined as those with an annual income of between Rs. 300,000 (4000 USD) and Rs. 600,000 (8000 USD); and middle-income households are those with an annual income of between Rs. 600,000 and Rs. 1,200,000 (8000–16,000 USD). The maximum living areas for the finished houses start from 30 square metres for very poor people, up to 160 square metres for middle-income households.

On 20 April 2020, the PMAY website stated that finance for 10 million homes had been sanctioned and about one-third of this number had actually been built. This is of course a remarkable achievement in the fairly brief period of five years, but it is all too possible that the subsidies will in due course generate their own demand, so that ever-increasing numbers of people will expect the government to take over an increasing proportion of the cost of their accommodation.

This is not the place to debate whether India should reverse its transition towards a free market economy, which was initiated by Finance Minister Manmohan Singh after the country's close call with total economic collapse. The PMAY does not appear to be part of or to presage such a move, and we should probably assume that it is more in the nature of a one-off populist move. This assumption is based on the fact that the entire programme relies on either direct or interest subsidies. The work involved in enabling an affordable housing market is unresolved. If this is correct, we would argue that the present trend towards making markets work for the poor rather than replacing them with subsidy and state control is likely to continue, and that housing policy should move in the directions we have outlined rather than towards increased subsidy.

It is always possible to argue that people cannot and will not change, but we found that the actors in Raipur's low-cost housing world are making conscious rather than conditioned choices. The slum dwellers are not a homogeneous population. They differ in their economic capacities, their occupations, their gender, their castes, and their regional origins. They have different needs, such as rickshaw drivers who prefer to live where public transport is not readily available, and different preferences, such as some households who prefer to stay in the slum even when they could afford to pay for a regular home, whereas others want to move out of the slum as soon as possible.

Their political affiliations are also different. Some vote on the basis of long-term patronage relationships, while others 'shop around' for the 'best deal' to solve a particular problem. Promises work on trust, and the politician who fails to deliver on a promise loses their base of voters. The slum dwellers have to explain what they need, appraise the services they can get in return for their vote, to approach opposition leaders for better deals, participate in mass protests, and generally engage in a complex process, with every move involving a cost and a cost–benefit analysis.[12]

The politicians also have to make choices: they are reluctant to change the 'system' because they know that the outcomes are uncertain, and they are unwilling to take this risk. The politicians of the dominant political party in Chhattisgarh, which had been voted into power for three consecutive terms by 2012, had a winning formula. They recognised the need to change to a market model for low-cost housing, but they were reluctant to change the way political decisions are being made because it serves their purpose. As one politician admitted to us, they believe that change will have to come from the voters; if their electorate starts to demand change, they will be forced to oblige (Interviewee-3F).

These decisions may seem irrational or merely lazy, but it is clear that the actors are being rational. They are making their choices in culturally accepted ways, constrained by the institutional structures in which they find themselves. Institutions constrain behaviour, and the institutions may have to be changed before behaviours will change.

Therefore, any changes that are made in order to introduce a market for low-cost housing must be sufficiently attractive to persuade the various actors to change from a clientelist political system to a market system. How can a change be introduced that would make the actors who benefit from the current clientelist system voluntarily move to a market system?

It may be impossible to convince all the actors that such a change would be for the better; there will be winners and losers. Clientelism relationships are mediated by brokers, who are therefore the most obvious losers. In Raipur, they are the local councillors (or *Parshad*). The city politicians would also lose from the change to a market system, but it would not necessarily put a total end to clientelism, so the patrons, the clients, and the brokers might be able to move on to other goods and services for such exchanges.

Seventy-four percent of the people whom we surveyed could afford to buy their own dwelling, and this figure excludes the one-fifth of the slum dwellers who earned more than the qualification limits set for the urban poor in India. Slum dwellers who cannot afford the market cost of formal housing will need alternative arrangements. If such arrangements are not put in place, then they will be worse off if the clientelist system stops.

The most obvious winners would be the households who are able and willing to buy low-cost homes from the formal market, and the developers who would supply the dwellings. The change would also benefit financial institutions, construction workers, building material producers, and other auxiliary industries related to housing.

The state-level ministers might or not benefit. If they fail to create an affordable market, and they stop the practice of clientelism in the process, they would lose the votes of the slum dwellers. However, if the change was successful, it would improve the image of the state-level ministers in charge of Housing and Urban Development, as well as that of the Chief Minister.

The most visible political effect of such a change would be its impact on the way that political decisions are made and resources are allocated. There would be a shift from the clientelist distribution of resources to a programmatic one, where the criteria and rules of the distribution are public, and actually determine the distribution, rather than doing so only in theory (Stokes et al., 2013). The benefits would not depend on the individuals' or groups' political support, nor would they go to party members, voters, or individuals. The process would cease to be private and undisclosed but would be open and radically different from the current practice. It would therefore be subject to comments and criticism from political opponents and open to the scrutiny of the electorate.

All these issues would have to be taken into account when a formal market for low-cost housing was being developed. This process will be explored, and the responsible actors will be discussed, under our recommendations in Chapter 7.

Notes

1 A Mimeograph quoted in WIEGO (n.d.); Bhowmik (2001)
2 7/30 developers (23.3%)
3 11/30 developers (36.6%)
4 The Administrative Reforms Commission (ARC) is the committee appointed by the Government of India for giving recommendations for reviewing the public administration system of India. The first ARC was established on 5 January 1966. The Second ARC was constituted on 31 August 2005, for preparing a detailed blueprint for revamping the public administrative system.
5 The Government of India nationalised the 14 largest commercial banks in 1969, and six more in 1980. In the early 1990s, the government embarked on a policy of liberalisation, licensing a small number of private banks. Today, there are government banks, private banks, and foreign banks. However, they are all regulated by the RBI to various extents.
6 *Nagar Palika* = Municipal Corporation
7 See Gnaneshwar (1995) and Baken (2003)
8 Comparison of per capita spending on urban capital expenditure on services (water, sewage, city roads, storm water drains, mass transit, solid waste, and low-income housing) for financial year 2007–2008.
9 See Document Ref: No.N-11025/40/2010-UCD (MoHUPA, GoI, 2012)
10 See Stokes et al. (2013)
11 See Press Trust India (2012), Prasad K. (2014), Express News Service (2014), and Aiyar (2008) for reports on "loan pardoning" in India.
12 As Taylor-Robinson (2010) argues in her study, some of these measures, like mass protest, can become very costly for those involved, particularly if the state responds with violence.

7

CAN THERE BE A MARKET FOR AFFORDABLE HOUSING IN CHHATTISGARH?

Our central questions in this book were: *What are the factors that constrain the market for affordable housing?* and *Can any of the institutions which constrain the market be altered in such a way that a market is formed?* The previous chapters have attempted to answer these questions. In this final chapter, we draw some conclusions and make some recommendations, which we hope will help to restructure the system.

It is generally believed that low-income people in India live in slums because they cannot afford to buy or rent decent dwellings. As mentioned earlier, studies from as far back as the late 1990s have shown that many of the people who live in slums can afford to pay a significant amount for housing, such as through a monthly rent, and they can also pay for services such as water and garbage disposal.

It was not clear, however, whether they could actually buy a house. This was because earlier studies did not take the institutional context into account: they failed to consider the possibilities that under a different set of institutions, the costs of housing might be reduced and slum households might get access to credit. These studies focussed only on how much money the households were able and willing to spend every month on water, pay toilets, or other civic services. The slum households had no access to credit; hence, the studies did not ask whether or not the households could afford an initial deposit and the monthly instalments at market interest rates.

We therefore explored whether there is the potential market for low-cost housing, and if there is, why formal private sector institutions do not try to satisfy it. The notion that it is not sufficiently profitable for private builders is partly based on the belief that slum dwellers cannot afford to pay the cost of such housing. However, this belief ignores the impact of institutional structures on markets and how this can affect market outcomes. An alternative approach was taken to find out whether the existing institutional structures prevent the emergence of a market for low-cost housing in Raipur; if they do, it then it follows that alternative institutional arrangements could facilitate such a market.

In order to investigate this question, we asked whether low-income people who live in the slums could pay the full cost of affordable housing. As described in Chapter 5, we found that about three-fourths of our sample of 211 households from 21 slums in Raipur said they could afford to do so; we consider them to be prospective customers for affordable homes. We assessed their ability to buy using two hypothetical 'model' house designs, the cost of which was estimated by experienced builders. We assumed that they would have to pay an initial deposit of 20% and monthly instalments for 20 years at the market interest rate of 12% for housing loans.

Research in other urban areas in India supports this finding. Monitor Deloitte, in its 2013 industry report on *State of the Low Income Housing Market in India*, states that a typical household[1] can afford a house costing up to 40 times their monthly income. Using this metric, the lower-income and poorest people could afford to buy a house costing between Rs. 600,000 and 1,000,000 (8000 USD–13,500 USD) and Rs. 400,000 to 600,000 (5000 USD–8000 USD), respectively. This report was based on studies in other cities that were carried out somewhat earlier than our research, but their conclusions are in line with our findings.

Our next step was to find out whether it was possible to build the 'hypothetical house' of 300 square feet for the poorest people for the cost of Rs. 300,000 (4000 USD). We investigated this through random interviews of 30 developers and builders who work in Raipur. Their approximate estimates of the cost of building a 300-square-foot home[2] came to an average of Rs. 400,000, or 5000 USD. This estimate was based on the government regulations for this type of house and was more than what the poorest families had said they could afford.

However, under a different set of regulations, as described in Chapter 3, the builders estimated that the cost could be reduced by over one-quarter, to just under Rs. 300,000 (or 4000 USD), including their profit. The suggested changes in the regulations included higher densities, reducing the double taxation by considering building to be only an industry and not an industry as well as a service, allowing larger-scale and thus more efficient projects, and including transferable development rights that builders can use for their own higher-cost housing projects or can sell to other builders. These changes would make it profitable to build the model houses. This, along with the fact that an NGO in Raipur was said by one of our interviewees to be building similar dwellings at prices well under Rs. 300,000 (or 4000 USD) led us to conclude that our 'hypothetical houses' could actually be built.

Additional changes, such as faster approvals and transparent online procedures that would reduce the builders' transaction costs, could bring the cost down further. If there was an adequate supply of serviced land for low-cost housing for, say, five years, the transaction costs that the builders incur in searching for and verifying the land for development would be further reduced.

Industry reports (Agarwal, Jain, & Karamchandani, 2013) agree that "given current land and construction costs, it is possible for private builders to build houses at these price-points (Rs. 400,000–600,000) and cater to a housing market of 13–15 million units which could be worth between Rs.

8500 and Rs. 9500 billion, or 113 to 127 billion USD". A substantial number of the slum population could afford to buy a house, and builders can profitably build decent and affordable housing. Given that there is the potential for an affordable and profitable market in low-cost housing, it is clear that non-economic constraints are preventing the emergence of such a market.

The government recognises that the current situation is unacceptable; some changes have been made, but they have had little impact. This 'institutional inertia' can be explained by reference to the culture of clientelism which pervades Indian politics.

Our survey indicated that although many households could, in principle, afford to buy a decent house if it were available, many would choose not to. Some said that they did not want to lose the community of the slum neighbourhood which serves them well for free childcare and also helps to defend their interests. They also said that if they bought their own house, they might lose the possibility of getting a free house in case their slum was cleared, and if their slum is not cleared, they still hope that basic services might be provided in their slum through a slum upgrading project. This would be a good deal for some households, as their present informal property is larger than they would be able to afford in the market.

Slum dwellers who can access credit would lose the possibility of getting one of the admittedly scarce houses which are being built by government agencies, whose price is subsidised and therefore lower than for a house of the same standard built commercially. They also realise that there is a good chance that a housing loan might at some time be waived as part of a political campaign. In general, our respondents distrust private builders, and they realise that they could not be sure of getting a loan. Also, some said that they could not afford the time to search for a house or pay the bribes which are necessary for registration.

All these reasons, apart from slum dwellers' reluctance to lose their neighbours, can be considered to be institutional constraints.

Institutional constraints also affect the builders. They cannot build homes at an affordable price, not because of costs of construction and land but because of the lack of appropriate serviced land. Government agencies build low-cost houses and sell them below cost, and thus damage the market. Private builders have to pay high interest rates on loans, there is a shortage of labour because government schemes discourage rural–urban migration, and they fear that there will not be enough demand because poorer people cannot access credit. In addition, the slow approval process increases transaction costs, and they have to pay two lots of taxes as well as bribes. The lack of properly documented and secure property rights adds to the time and thus the cost, and the regulations require that low-cost houses should be allotted rather than being sold, and they also limit the density of housing. This makes land even more scarce, and thus pushes up the costs even more.

Decisive government action could address most of those constraints, as the builders and others told us, but politicians are often reluctant to take the necessary action. Because their ministries are short of money, they want to work on highly visible projects which will increase their chances of getting re-elected. Such projects can be new housing developments, but there are far too few of these to satisfy the demand. If a genuine market emerges, the clientelist system will be weakened, and politicians may lose their power. This would also entail the loss of the power and money which is a part of the corrupt government machinery; the present organisational structure and division of responsibilities would have to be changed radically, and that would weaken the positions of politicians and government officials.

In Chapter 6, we showed how clientelism supports institutional inertia, and we argued that because the actors are rational, a genuine market for low-cost housing might bring about the desired changes if it offered enough advantages to most of the parties concerned. We concluded that clientelism is an alternative to the market; the actors make rational political and economic decisions within the constraints of the institutional setup. It follows that if the institutional structures are changed, the actors will make different choices. Some actors might gain, and others would lose from the change, and there would be political consequences. However, the ease with which the institutional structure can be changed would depend on how deeply entrenched the clientelism is, and who are the actors most threatened by the changes.

The need for change is recognised, but the situation is not changing. The formal institutional structure can be deliberately changed, but the outcome of such change will depend on social approval, and on less informal social institutions. A genuine market in low-cost housing is more likely to be created if the process of formal institutional change is accompanied by informal brokering among the prospective buyers and sellers, involving the facilitators, to come to an acceptable set of terms for such a market. There will necessarily be winners and losers, and it will also be necessary to negotiate some form of compensation for those who might not gain from the change.

We have some initial recommendations, which are based on a deliberate 'design' for the market. However, given the institutional complexities and the uncertain outcome, this cannot be a straightforward process. Our recommendations are no more than an outline. Creating a market needs an evolutionary approach that can cope with uncertain outcomes. It will only be possible to find acceptable solutions to the problems that will arise if the process is effectively mediated.

Our research has concluded that a new market for low-cost housing can only emerge if certain premises are accepted. The government cannot afford to provide enough low-cost housing, and private investment will be needed. There are potential sources of supply and demand for low-cost housing, and a significant number of low-income people are able and willing to buy their own homes; a high proportion of low-income people in the slums own their own homes, and they wish to continue to do so.

A market could provide more choice of location and design as well as meeting basic requirements, and there is a need for faster housing development to keep up with the pace of urbanisation. In general, housing is a key growth driver for the economy, and many studies correlate housing and infrastructure investments in the formal sector with a nation's gross national product.

We have concluded that the market for low-cost housing will need to be deliberately designed and developed. This will involve restructuring the existing government supply system rather than merely overlaying new policies on the existing organisational structure. The new system will have to satisfy certain conditions. It will only apply to new houses which are built for owner occupation, and the houses will have to conform to the standards for low-cost housing in terms of their size and the availability of the five basic amenities – toilets, drinking water, electricity, drainage, and access roads. If plots of land have to be pooled or restructured, the existing residents will have priority.

The prices of the houses should be competitive with local house prices, and the government must ensure an adequate supply of serviced land and must allow higher density limits for low-cost housing. It will also be necessary to provide finance to credit-worthy buyers and to the builders, to whom it may be necessary to offer lower interest rates for low-cost housing projects in order to encourage investment. The approval procedures will also have to be made faster and more transparent, and it will also be important to make improvements to the supply of serviced land. The supply of this land, the faster approvals, and the credit will have to be conditional on the houses being sold to low-income families; this rule will have to be enforced through collaboration with homeowners in the neighbourhood. It is also important that the houses are sold through an open market and are not allotted by the government.

What is being proposed is a market-based housing supply system which is similar to the current system for the supply of high- and middle-cost housing. Figure 7.1 illustrates this system and shows the institutions that affect housing provision either directly or indirectly. Both systems are influenced by the state through the same housing policy, tax, and employment institutions, as well as the planning system and state infrastructure expenditure. The difference lies in their impact on housing supply.

The supply system for low-income housing will have to address the institutional constraints which we have identified. Figure 7.2 illustrates the supply system for low-cost housing which we propose. It is similar to the present informal system; they are both market-based, but the difference lies in the good being traded, which is a 'decent' low-cost house with the five basic facilities and clear legal title.

It is beyond the scope of this book to propose the best way to address each constraint, as this would require the state and central governments to

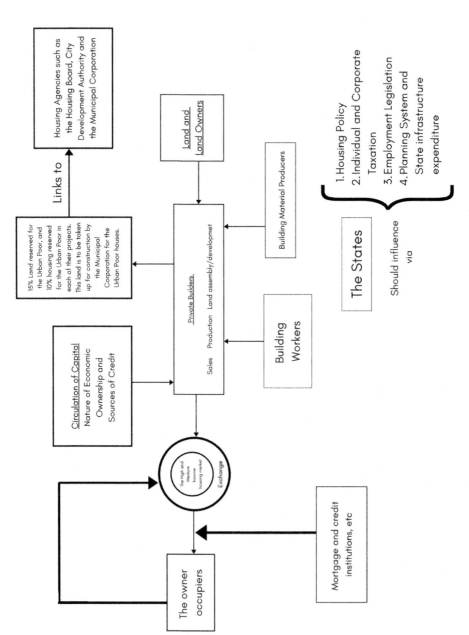

Figure 7.1 Current supply system for higher- and middle-cost housing in Raipur with links to the government system

Source: All figures in this chapter are authors' constructions

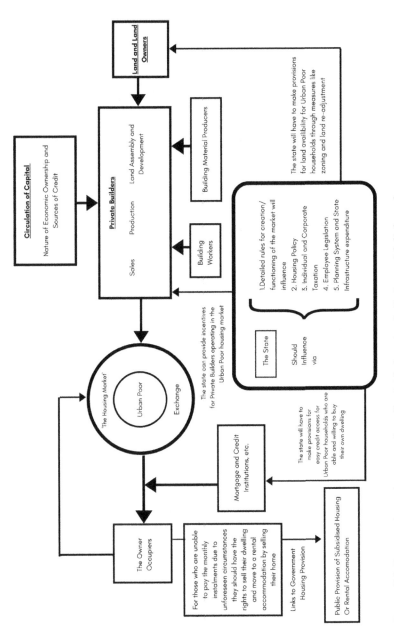

Figure 7.2 Proposed supply system for affordable housing in Raipur with link to the government system

allocate resources appropriately and to consider the overall political implications. We are proposing a totally new structure of housing provision.

In order to be a facilitator rather than a principal actor in the affordable housing market, the state government will have to limit its own provision to those who are unable to buy such housing. It will not be easy to demarcate this group. One option would be to provide communal-style housing with common kitchens and toilets, which would not be attractive to people who can afford low-cost homes on the private market. It might be possible to fix an income threshold below which a household would be unable to afford a low-cost house in the private market, but this would be difficult to manage. A family whose income was above the limit might have other expenses such as a large family, medical emergencies, or other social commitments, and would thus not be able to afford the down payment or the monthly payments – and would therefore be eligible for the low-cost housing provision.

Links between supply systems in partially segregated housing segments

The various housing supply systems in Raipur which are illustrated in Chapters 6 and 7 are linked to each other, as shown in Figure 7.3. The shaded boxes highlight the links that we found between the various segments of the housing market. If the systems are segregated according to the income groups they serve, there should be three systems: one for people who cannot afford to buy their own houses, which will be serviced by the government; one to serve people who are the focus of our study, who can afford to buy but are unable to do so because of institutional constraints, and need a market-based system which will address these constraints; and the existing market-based system for better-off people. The same housing suppliers may work in more than one system, or new suppliers may come in to service the new market, but the operating rules within each system must be applied uniformly. Different suppliers operating in the same system must be governed by the same rules. This does not mean that other suppliers such as NGOs or housing cooperatives should not be allowed to provide low-cost housing; only that they should not be able to sell below the market price. If subsidised housing is provided for people who do not need subsidies and are able and willing to afford their own homes, this diverts limited resources from those who are genuinely in need of subsidy.

Because there will be several housing supply systems operating in the same city, the system for low-cost housing must in some ways be linked to the systems for other types of housing; the markets cannot and should not be totally separate. For example, a developer who builds lower-density homes for better-off clients could also be entitled to transferable development rights, which would be an incentive to build for lower-income clients. Households might also want to be able to move from one supply system to another as their financial situation changes.

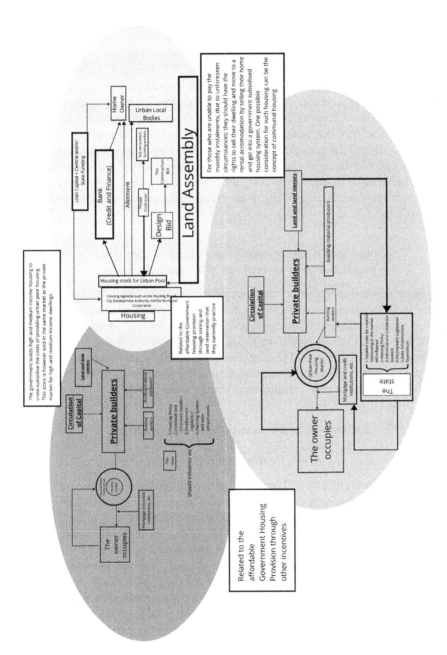

Figure 7.3 Proposed interconnected housing supply system for Raipur

A housing supply system can in theory work on its own, but it is also part of a much larger entity, which is a system of partially segregated housing markets. If a new market-based system is created, it will have to be linked to the existing systems, as shown in Figure 7.3, depending on how the different market segments influence each other. The three individual systems are illustrated in Figures 6.1, 6.2, and 7.2. Figure 7.3 shows only an indication of the separate systems and is focussed on the boxes which show the links between them, which are also shown in the diagrams of the individual systems. In practice, there will be many links between the various systems, so that if a new system is created for low-cost housing, it will also affect the existing markets for middle- and higher-income housing. A new market will have to overcome the existing barriers and constraints but will also have to be governed by a detailed set of regulations based on an in-depth understanding of the context, operations, and requirements of the market.

Some initial recommendations for restructuring market supply system for affordable housing

We have some initial policy recommendations; these do not take many issues into account, such as labour markets, the political implications of slum clearance and redevelopment, social welfare, local economic development, and others which will have to be considered when the new policy is planned and implemented. These recommendations focus on the introduction of new institutions and practices, their compliance with market regulations, and how these new conditions might be introduced.

Introducing new institutions and practices

National level

The national government will have to change its rules so that state governments are allowed to channel their resources to avoid conflict with the creation and functioning of the market for low-cost housing.

We suggest that the government should make it clear that slums consist of households with varying needs, so there should not be one policy for the entire slum population. They should also explain that the current policy of providing infrastructure such as roads, drainage, and water in a slum that has already developed in a haphazard way is an inefficient and unsustainable use of land. They should introduce land-pooling, with priority for the existing occupants of the land. The government's primary responsibility should be to provide housing for those who cannot afford the cost of their own homes; the critical fact to be recognised is that many if not most slum dwellers can afford to pay for their own housing.

If free housing is provided as part of a slum clearance programme, slum dwellers who are willing and able to pay for their housing will be unwilling to move; hence, subsidised or free accommodation should only be provided for people who cannot afford to buy their own housing. They should be provided with communal housing or single-family rentals as part of an affordable rental scheme, such as was suggested by the government in 2013. Those who cannot even afford to rent their homes should be given access to night shelters. The process of moving from communal housing to single-family rentals to owner-occupied homes creates a clear incentive for households to move up the housing ladder. This allows households to move up or down the ladder as their circumstances change.

State level

At the state level, there are several organisations which provide low-cost housing, but none of them 'owns' the obligation to ensure 'affordable housing for all' as is enshrined in the housing policy of the state of Chhattisgarh. There should therefore be a new state-level public sector body which is responsible for enabling a market for low-cost homes, while other agencies such as the State Housing Board continue to provide housing for those who cannot afford to pay for it themselves.

This new organisation should mediate and negotiate between the various actors in the housing market and work towards an informal consensus about the rules which will govern the market. This will require meetings with slum dwellers to understand their needs and aspirations, and to identify the assurances that will be necessary for them. There will also need to be consultations with builders in order to understand the conditions they will need to enable them to operate in the new market, as well as discussions with the various facilitating agencies – such as financial institutions and government bodies – in order to estimate the resources that will have to be made available for monitoring and enforcement, as well as arbitration and conflict resolution. The new negotiating agency will have to fix, in principle, the terms under which the market for affordable housing will function in a socially acceptable way that can be facilitated by the state. Based on this informal consensus, the new agency will also have to set guidelines for market operations, while the state government will have to decide how and at what level the various constraints will be addressed.

City level

It is not possible to set income limits for which households can or cannot afford to pay for their housing at the level of India as a whole or even one state; this will have to be determined at the city level. This will only be an approximate guideline to determine who is eligible for subsidised housing, as people should be able to determine for themselves what kind of dwelling suits their needs and their capacity to pay. If they say they need government-subsidised housing, they will have to prove that they cannot afford to pay the market cost, and a new organisation will have to be created at the city level to monitor and enforce the new rules and to arbitrate and resolve conflicts when necessary.

Even when the constraints to the provision of low-cost housing have been addressed so that it can be a profitable business, there will still be a tendency for builders to operate in the most profitable market, and the profit per unit will usually be lower for affordable homes. There will thus be a need to incentivise the market, by specifying certain areas where only low-cost homes can be built, or by providing other incentives such as permission for large-scale projects which will benefit from economies of scale. These rules and incentives will have to be set at the city level.

Compliance with the new market regulations

Will the government be able to enforce the new market rules, once they have been determined? The government only has limited resources for monitoring and enforcement, so the new markets must generally be self-regulating and transparent. It will also be important to ensure that all parties informally agree to the rules of the new market before they are formally drafted. Like any market, this will provide a platform where two or more parties who voluntarily agree to do business can complete their transactions. The rules will be framed in order to protect all parties and to allow for fair exchange. If rules are considered to be fair, and the enforcing authorities are believed to be legitimate, there is a greater likelihood of compliance.

How these conditions might be introduced

It will take time to reach an informal consensus, but if it can be done, it will be an indication that the various parties approve of the rules of the new market and will encourage them to comply. The slum dwellers can be represented by some form of social group from the community, or possibly by an NGO that works with them and can consult them and voice their concerns. In 2001, a similar situation occurred in Mumbai when the government, a private builder, and an NGO that represented the slum dwellers were involved in negotiating several issues. The slum dwellers eventually bypassed the NGO and made a deal with the builder which was acceptable to the state (Sanyal & Mukhija, 2001). It might also be possible for the Chhattisgarh Real Estate Developers Association (CREDAI-CG) to represent the builders, while the financial institutions and the relevant government departments should be involved as needed. The whole process should be facilitated by the state government organisation which we have suggested should be tasked with enabling the new market.

This change will require considerable political will. It will also involve a major political risk, as it will require politicians to downplay immediate short-term solutions in favour of a long-term promise to create a market for low-cost homes. This change may alter slum dwellers' expectations from the political parties, which will no longer promise immediate tangible benefits such as short-term grants and subsidies. These are some of the higher-level governance issues that will need to be addressed.

If the government implements these recommendations, it should be able to address the various constraints in a coordinated way. There are many ways in which the constraints can be resolved, and there will have to be a political debate in order to evaluate and plan the way forward. Decisions will have to be made on the allocation of resources between states and the central government, as well as the economic and political implications for other sectors. If the market for low-cost housing is restructured, and an institution is set up whose only function will be to facilitate the market, then all the actors involved in the system will be aware of each other's roles. It will then be clear who is responsible for creating and maintaining the rules, rather than the responsibility being lost in a multitude of different institutions, policies, and schemes.

Institutions are not always visible; they may be no more than shared concepts in the minds of participants. It is often difficult to identify institutions of this kind, or to assess their strength and capacity.

In any effort to improve or create institutions, it is always important to be clear about the context in which they operate. If the institutional constraints to supply and demand are addressed, this will not inevitably result in the creation of an effective market. We have tried to isolate each segment of the market mechanism so that homes can be provided for that segment by identifying the actors which operate in the market and the institutions which govern it. In Chhattisgarh, developers cater to multiple markets. If a builder gets transferable development rights to build high-cost housing, this can be a strong incentive to enter the low-income housing market elsewhere.

Most analyses of housing markets assume that there is one kind of provider for one market, and that all the suppliers are governed by the same set of rules when operating within the same market segment. But in India, there are several providers for the same market, and they operate under different conditions. They have different advantages and different constraints. For example, housing cooperatives may get low-cost credit, NGOs get tax exemptions, and government agencies get subsidised land or other benefits. So while they do compete in the same market and influence each other, they cannot be considered as one group of suppliers. Each type of supplier has to use different ways of acquiring land and finance. It is not useful to analyse these different types of supplier as if they were all operating under the same conditions. One way to overcome this problem is to consider the market segment for each type of house separately but also as being linked to the other segments in one coherent entity, as is illustrated in Figure 7.3. Alternatively, the total market can be subdivided into different sub-markets according to the type of housing provider and can then be merged with others to identify the ways in which they influence each other.

NGO studies of slums are based on the single perspective of the slum dwellers. Industry reports take the builders' perspective, and government-sponsored reports naturally take governments' perspective. We hope that we have considered all three perspectives and have thus come up with solutions which are feasible from all three points of view.

Our study aimed to show how the problem of providing low-cost housing could be approached more holistically, rather than to provide all the information that will be necessary to solve the problem.

Some of the variables have therefore been dealt with in a very simple way. Transaction costs, for instance, were calculated in terms of the number of days spent in getting approvals. Similarly, the effect of institutional constraints on the supply of low-cost housing was assessed by asking builders whether they were actually prevented from entering the market, and the constraints on demand were calculated by counting the number of households who said that they faced each constraint. Slum dwellers, builders, and the government all had to be covered, and it was not easy to quantify the effects of transaction costs and property rights on the market.

Many cultural factors are themselves, in a sense, institutions and they are especially important in India's caste-conscious society, where caste differences affect market decisions. In Raipur, for example, some slum dwellers refused to be relocated into free houses because one so-called 'untouchable' caste that rear pigs were first allotted a set of houses in that block. The remaining houses are still vacant. It was important for our study to engage with the wider social context of the policy-making process, and any attempt to make fundamental changes in the low-cost housing market should do the same. We had to accept, for example, rather less precision than we would have liked in our survey, and thus had more time for informal conversations with each household.

We were engaged in an 'academic' study, but we believe that our socio-anthropological approach made it possible to identify and interpret the views of slum dwellers, builders, government officials, and other stakeholders in ways which have important practical implications.

We identified a number of factors, for instance, which might usually be considered too obvious to state, and we were also able to elicit concerns that respondents might be reluctant to share in a public consultation. Our informal approach also enabled us to talk informally to other people who were not part of our sample of respondents but who mentioned factors which we might otherwise have missed.

Some final points

India has something between 65 and 90 million people who live in sub-standard urban accommodation (*Times of India* 11 October 2011), which means that the country is home to the world's largest population of slum dwellers. This sad situation is the result of the country's shortage of decent low-cost housing.

Our study was carried out in Raipur, a medium-sized city in the state of Chhattisgarh in central India, and we cannot of course claim for certain that our findings apply to other Indian cities. There is no reason to suppose, however, that the situation in Raipur is radically different from elsewhere. Our study has revealed a number of features of the demand and supply aspects of the market for low-cost housing which suggest that the slum problem can be significantly alleviated.

Our results challenge the neo-liberal theory of enabling markets that was earlier promoted by The World Bank (1993). According to this view, when there is a potential, a market will emerge through deregulation and privatisation. Our findings reject this, and they show that many constraints arise from informal institutions, and hence cannot be addressed only by changing formal institutions.

Our findings also relate to the approach that was also suggested by The World Bank (2000), which suggested that the critical institutional constraints of land, credit, and transaction costs – which prevent the emergence of markets – could be addressed individually. We have shown that institutional constraints are not independent of each other, and that a market will not necessarily emerge if the constraints are addressed individually. The constraints may have arisen because the formal and informal institutions have interacted to form a structure or complex of institutions that jointly inhibit change, so the constraints must be addressed together.

We have also demonstrated that it is vital to understand the social context in order to be able to analyse the roles of different institutions and to introduce changes. Mixed-income housing development systems that work well in other countries such as the United States did not work in Raipur, and the government was forced to change the zoning laws to suit the local social context. Transplanting institutions, without regard for the social acceptance of such regulations, cannot be successful.

The same housing policy cannot be applied to all slum dwellers. Slums include households with varying levels of ability to afford homes, and with different needs and aspirations. Many slum dwellers are willing and able to buy their own homes. The low-cost housing is not independent of markets for other types of housing. Policymakers must therefore consider the influence of one housing market segment on the other. The various markets, the formal and informal institutions, and the constraints which affect them must be systematically examined. It is not enough only to address the constraints.

The market for low-cost housing must be designed and structured with detailed rules and regulations to frame its operations. Housing problems can only be solved with a multi-pronged approach, but one approach may easily hinder another. Slum upgrading and subsidised housing, for example, can inhibit the development of markets.

We do not claim that our conclusions and suggestions for change can in themselves solve the problem of low-cost housing provision in India, in Chhattisgarh, or even in Raipur. We do believe, however, that we have uncovered some fundamental and previously neglected issues which can, if they are addressed, lead to very significant improvements.

Clearly, the way ahead will not be simple, and it has been easier to write down our suggestions for change than it will be to implement them. But we believe that if the present way in which low-cost housing is provided – or more often, not provided – is continued, then the problem of the growth of unregulated, unhealthy, and inhumane slums will continue and expand. Radical changes are needed, and our findings point the way towards them.

Change can begin at any time, in parts of Raipur, or elsewhere in Chhattisgarh, or other states in India – and it is urgent. Numerous questions remain unanswered, but they can be addressed at the same time as practical steps can be taken to alleviate the international disgrace of slums.

There are many different planning regulations and systems, and it is important to analyse them and to find out how they actually affect the market for low-cost housing. The opinions of slum dwellers themselves also need to be better understood. How do they view their rights as squatters? To what extent does the possibility, however remote, that they might be entitled to a free home if their slum is cleared create an incentive to stay in the slum, and what difference does the length of time someone has lived in a slum make to their sense of entitlement to free or subsidised housing? It has to be understood that this 'right' to a free house is not a legal entitlement but a political favour, which has been obtained in the same way as the 'right' to squat. The interface between legal entitlement and informal rights, which have been obtained through political clientelism rather than any form of market, needs to be better understood.

The government's capacity is limited in India, as in most other low-income countries, and as a result, any solutions to the problem of low-cost housing must take account of this weakness. Regulations of foreign origin cannot be used without taking this into account. Raghuram Rajan, Governor of the Reserve Bank of India between 2013 and 2016, said "Change is risky, but as India develops, not changing is even riskier". If the situation continues unchanged, the problems of poorer Indians who live in slums will get worse. The growing slum population is an enormous social, humanitarian, and environmental problem. A large proportion of the slum dwelling population are both able and willing to buy their own decent homes. If this fact is recognised, and appropriate steps are taken, India's and indeed the world's slum problem will be significantly reduced.

Notes

1 Housing Affordability has to be always measured on a sliding scale, as two families with the same income but with different family size might not have the same affordability.
2 This was a rough estimate, as nearly one-fourth of the cost of building a house was the cost of land, which varies widely.

REFERENCES

Abrams, C. (1964). *Man's struggle for shelter in an urbanizing world*. Cambridge, MA: MIT Press.

Abrams, C. (1966). *Squatter settlements: The problem and the opportunity* (No. 63). Washington, DC: Office of International Affairs, Department of Housing and Urban Development.

Accountability Initiative. (2014). *Accountability review*. JNNURM, GOI, 2013–14.

ADB. (2006, updated 21 October 2013). *ADB project data sheet*. Manila: Asian Development Bank.

Agarwal, A., Jain, V., & Karamchandani, A. (2013). *State of the low income housing market: Encouraging progress & opportunity to realize dreams of millions*. Monitor Inclusive Markets, India. Deloitte Touche Tohmatsu India Private Limited.

Aggarwal, S. (2008, September 30). *Liquid debt*. New Delhi: Down to Earth, Society for Environmental Communications.

Aiyar, S. (2008, March 9). *Loan waiver: Not an election winner*. Retrieved June 10, 2014, from http://swaminomics.org/loan-waiver-not-an-election-winner/

Allen, D. W. (2000). Transaction costs. In B. Bouckaert & G. De Geest (Eds.), *Encyclopedia of law and economics, Volume I: The history and methodology of law and economics* (pp. 893–926). Cheltenham, Northampton: Edward Elgar Publishing Limited.

Angel, S., & Boonyabancha, S. (1988). Land sharing as an alternative to eviction. *Third World Planning Review, 10*(2).

Arrow, K. J. (1969). The organization of economic activity: issues pertinent to the choice of market versus nonmarket allocation. *The analysis and evaluation of public expenditure: the PPB system, 1*, 59-73.

Askaribank. (2015). *Askari home musharakah*. Retrieved May 13, 2015, from www. askaribank.com.pk/islamic_musharakah.php

Atuahene, B. (2004). *Legal title to land as an intervention against urban poverty in developing nations*. Retrieved March 7, 2013, from The George Washington International Law Review, George Washington University National Law Center. HighBeam Research: www.highbeam.com/doc/1P3-779945941.html

Bacharach, S. B., & Lawler, E. J. (1981). *Bargaining: Power, tactics and outcomes*. San Francisco, CA and London: Jossey-Bass Inc.

Baindur, V., & Kamath, L. (2009). *Reengineering urban infrastructure: World Bank & Asia Development Bank*. New Delhi: Bank Information Center (BIC).

Baken, R.-J. (2003). *Plotting, squatting, public purpose and politics: Land market development, low income housing and public intervention in India*. Hants: Ashgate Publishing Limited.

Baken, R.-J., & van der Linden, J. (1992). *Land delivery for low income groups in third world cities*. Hants: Ashgate Publishing Limited.

Ball, M. (1983). *Housing policy and economic power: The political economy of owner occupation*. London and New York: Methuen & Co. Ltd.

Banerjee, A. V., Cole, S., & Duflo, E. (2003). *Bank financing in India. A tale of two giants: India's and China's experience with reform and growth*. New Delhi: International Monetary Fund and the National Council of Applied Economic Research (India).

Banga, R., & Das, A. (2012). *Twenty years of India's liberalization: Experiences and lessons*. Geneva: United Nations (UNCTAD).

Bardhan, P. K. (1984). *The political economy of development in India* (pp. 185–205). Oxford: Basil Blackwell.

Bardhan, P. (1989). The new institutional economics and development theory: A brief critical assessment. *World Development, 17*(9), 1389–1395.

Barman, S., Sharma, A., & Dey, P. D. (2006, December). *Land tenure security: Is titling enough?* NIUA WP 06-03. New Delhi: National Institute of Urban Affairs.

Benjamin, S. (1999, April 4–6). *Land, productive slums, and urban poverty*. World Bank, 20. Retrieved from http://www.rrojasdatabank.info/wpover/benjamin.pdf

Berner, E. (2000). *Informal developers, patrons, and the state: Institutions and regulatory mechanisms in popular housing*. ESF/N-AERUS Workshop 'Coping with informality and illegality in human settlements in developing cities', Leuven.

Berner, E. (2001). Learning from informal markets: Innovative approaches to land and housing provision. *Development in Practice, 14*(1).

Bhadra, D., & Brandao, A. (1993). *Urbanization, agricultural development and land allocation* (No. WDP201, p. 1). World Bank Discussion Papers. Washington, DC: World Bank. Retrieved from http://documents1.worldbank.org/curated/en/396621468766781948/pdf/multi-page.pdf

Bharucha, N. (2013, September 9). *Bribe demands hold up building projects in Mumbai*. Retrieved June 10, 2014, from The Times of India, Mumbai Edition: http://timesofindia.indiatimes.com/city/mumbai/Bribe-demands-hold-up-building-projects-in-Mumbai/articleshow/22425281.cms?referral=PM

Bhattacharya, K. P. (1998). *Affordable housing and infrastructure in India*. New Delhi: Reliance Publishing House.

Bhowmik, S. K. (2001). *Street vendors in Mumbai*. Retrieved February 18, 2014, from www.udri.org/udri/MumbaiReader10/15%20Sharit%20K.%20Bhowmik%20-%20Street%20Vendors%20in%20Mumbai.pdf?phpMyAdmin=w6qdoDhnTY-UA44T6XZMtfF7FTd

Boonyabancha, S. (2001, October). Savings and loans: Drawing lessons from some experiences in Asia. *Environment & Urbanization, 13*(2).

Boudreaux, K. (2005). *The role of property rights as an institution: Implications for development policy*. Arlington, VA: Mercatus Center at George Mason University.

Bowden, P. (1990). NGOs in Asia: Issue in development. *Public Administration and Development, 10*(2), 141–152.

Breslau, D. (2013). Designing a market-like entity: Economics in the politics of market formation. *Social Studies of Science, 43*(6), 829–851.

149

Cao, J., & Keivani, R. (2013). The limits and potentials of the housing market enabling paradigm: An evaluation of China's housing policies from 1998 to 2011. *Housing* Studies, *29*(1), 44–68.

CASUMM. (2008). *Institutionalizing citizens' participation: An evaluation of the community participation law and the community participation fund.* Bangalore: Collaborative for the Advancement of the Study of Urbanism through Mixed Media.

CEPT. (2010). *Report of workshop on 'land tenure issues in slum free city planning'.* Ahmedabad: Centre for Urban Equity, Ahmedabad and Ministry of Housing and Urban Poverty Alleviation, GoI.

Chandramouli, D. C. (2011). *Housing stock, amenities & assets in slums – Census 2011.* New Delhi: Registrar General & Census Commissioner, India.

Chhattisgarh Housing Board (CGHB). (2007). *Housing revolution in Chhattisgarh: 3 years of Chhattisgarh Housing Board.* Chhattisgarh, India: Chhattisgarh Housing Board.

Chhattisgarh Land Revenue Code, 1959 as amended by Chhattisgarh Land Revenue Code (Amendment) Ordinance, 2008. (2010). Raipur: India Publishing Company.

CMHN & VNC. (2004). *Affordable housing cooperatives: Conditions and prospects in Chicago.* Chicago, IL: Chicago Mutual Housing Network (CMHN) and Center for Neighborhood and Community Improvement (VNC).

CMS Transparency. (2012). *CMS-India corruption study 2012: Expanding slums & growing corruption.* Press Release, December 7, 2012. Retrieved May 21, 2014, from CMS India: www.cmsindia.org/PressReleaseCMS_ICS_2012.pdf

Cushman & Wakefield. (2014). *Housing: The game changer leading to double-digit GDP growth.* Cushman & Wakefield Research Publication. Retrieved from http://www.cushwakeasia.com/emkt/2014/India/HousingReport/HousingTheGameChanger.pdf

Dalal, M. (2014, January 17). *REFILE-India to boost muni market.* Retrieved June 12, 2014, from www.reuters.com/article/2014/01/17/india-bonds-municipal-idUSL2N0KQ0IB20140117

Davis, M. (2007). *Planet of slums.* London and New York: Verso.

Demsetz, H. (1967). Toward a theory of property rights. *The American Economic Review, 57*(2), 347–359.

Desai, V., & Loftus, A. (2013). Speculating on slums: Infrastructural fixes in informal housing in the global South. *Antipode, 45*(4), 789–808.

De Soto, H. (2000). *The mystery of capital.* London: Black Swan.

deWit, J., & Berner, E. (2009). Progressive patronage? Municipalities, NGOs, CBOs and the limits to slum dwellers' empowerment. *Development and Change, 40*(5), 927–947.

Down to Earth. (2008, September 30). *Ask no questions, just pay the water bill.* New Delhi: Down to Earth.

The Economic Times. (2006, October 14). *IL&FS unveils Rs 3K-Cr infra financing facility.* Retrieved June 12, 2014, from The Economic Times: http://economictimes.indiatimes.com/news/news-by-industry/banking/finance/ilfs-unveils-rs-3k-cr-infra-financing-facility/articleshow/2171047.cms

Eggertsson, T. (1990). *Economic behavior and institutions.* New York: Cambridge University Press.

Ensminger, J. (1996). *Making a market: The institutional transformation of an African society.* Melbourne: Cambridge University Press.

Enterprise Community Partners. (2014). *Impact of affordable housing on families and communities: A review of the evidence base*. Columbia, MD: Enterprise Community Partners, Inc.

ESF/N-AERUS Workshop – Working group 1. (2000). *Report of the Working group 1 – Strengths and weaknesses of new urban forms generated by informality and illegality*. ESF/N-AERUS Workshop 'Coping with informality and illegality in human settlements in developing cities', 23–36 May, Leuven.

Express News Service. (2014, June 9). *Chandrababu Naidu is CM, acts first on loan waivers*. Retrieved June 10, 2014, from The Indian Express: http://indianexpress.com/article/india/politics/tdp-chandrababu-naidu-cm-andhra-pradesh/

Feedback Ventures. (2006). Chapter 4 – Basic services for the poor. In *Lucknow city development plan* (pp. 32–40). Lucknow: Feedback Ventures.

Freeman, A., Kiddle, C., & Whitehead, C. (2000). Defining affordability. In *Restructuring housing systems: From social to affordable housing?* (pp. 100–105). York: Joseph Rowntree Foundation.

Fritz, V., Katayama, R., & Simle, K. (2008). *Breaking out of inequality traps: Political economy considerations*. PREM Notes: Poverty. Washington, DC: The World Bank.

Gangopadhyay, P., & Nath, S. (2001). Bargaining, coalitions and local expenditure. *Urban Studies, 38*(13), 2379–2391.

Giddings, S. W. (2007). *Housing challenges and opportunities in Sub-Saharan Africa*. Washington, DC: International Housing Coalition (IHC).

Gnaneshwar, V. (1995). Urban policies in India: Paradoxes and predicaments. *Habitat International, 19*(3), 293–316.

GTZ ASEM. (2010). *Slum profile [Raipur]*. Alchemy Urban Systems (P) Ltd. (Alchemy), Bangalore Consortium for DEWATS Dissemination (CDD Society) Bangalore, CEPT Research & Development Unit (CRDU), Ahmedabad. Raipur: Report commissioned by GTZ for RMC.

Gulyani, S., & Bassett, E. M. (2007). Retrieving the baby from the bathwater: Slum upgrading in Sub-Saharan Africa. *Environment and Planning C: Government and Policy, 25*(4), 486–515.

Hårsman, B., & Quigley, J. M. (1991). Housing markets and housing institutions in a comparative context. In *Housing markets and housing institutions: An international comparison* (pp. 1–29). Dordrecht, The Netherlands: Springer.

Hartzok, A. (2003). *Securing land for people, not for profit*. Retrieved June 3, 2014, from UN-Habitat: http://ww2.unhabitat.org/campaigns/tenure/bboard/people.htm

Help to buy. (2015). Retrieved April 8, 2015, from Help to buy: www.cambridge.gov.uk/shared-ownership-scheme

Hodgson, G. M. (2006). What are institutions? *Journal of Economic Issues, XL*(1).

Hong, Y. H., & Needham, B. (Eds.). (2007). *Analyzing land readjustment: Economics, law and collective action*. Boston, MA: Lincoln Land Institute.

Hopkin, J. (2006, August 31–September 3). *Conceptualizing political clientelism: Political exchange and democratic theory*. Paper prepared for APSA annual meeting, Philadelphia. Panel 46-18 'Concept analysis: Unpacking clientelism. Governance and neoliberalism'.

HUD. (2015). *Affordable housing*. Retrieved April 22, 2015, from US Department of Housing and Urban Development: http://portal.hud.gov/hudportal/HUD?src=/program_offices/comm_planning/affordablehousing/

Hugi, A. (2012, September 13). *Transitions – India: Fighting graft at the grassroots.* Retrieved May 21, 2014, from Foreign Policy: http://transitions.foreignpolicy.com/posts/2012/09/13/india_fighting_graft_at_the_grassroots_0http://transitions.foreignpolicy.com/posts/2012/09/13/india_fighting_graft_at_the_grassroots_0

IDB. (2012). *Slum upgrading: Lessons learned from Brazil* (F. Magalhães & F. di Villarosa, Eds.). Washington, DC: Inter-American Development Bank.

Igel, B., & Srinivas, H. (1996). The co-option of low-income borrowers by informal credit suppliers: A credit delivery model for squatter housing. *Third World Planning Review, 18*(3), 287.

Iyer, K. (2012, January 24). *Construction industry needs 12 million skilled workers: CREDAI.* Retrieved December 24, 2012, from The SME Horizon – Construction News and Views: http://smehorizon.sulekha.com/construction-industry-needs-12-million-skilled-workers_construction-viewsitem_6736

Jain, V., Chennuri, S., & Karamchandani, A. (2016). *Informal housing, inadequate property rights understanding the needs of India's informal housing dwellers.* Retrieved from www.omidyar.com

Jamwal, N. (2006, August 31). *Urban myths* (pp. 26–34). New Delhi: Down to Earth.

Jones, G. A. (1996, May). The difference between truth and adequacy: (Re)joining Baken, van der Linden and Malpezzi. *Third World Planning Review, 18*(2).

Keivani, R., & Werna, E. (2001, February). Modes of housing provision in developing countries. *Progress in Planning, 55*(2).

Kirk, M. (2002). *Ensuring efficient land management in peri-urban areas* (pp. 1–31). World Bank research reports: A review-in-process. Retrieved from http://documents1.worldbank.org/curated/en/485171468309336484/pdf/multi0page.pdf

Knight, J. (1992). *Institutions and social conflict.* Cambridge, New York, and Melbourne: Cambridge University Press.

Kumar, V., & Pandit, R. K. (2013, March). Indian urban development planning approach. *International Journal of Engineering Science and Innovative Technology (IJESIT), 2*(2).

Libecap, G. D. (2008). Transaction costs, property rights, and the tools of the new institutional economics: Water rights and water markets. In E. Brousseau & J.-M. Glachant (Eds.), *New institutional economics: A guidebook* (pp. 272–291). New York: Cambridge University Press.

Mahadevia, J., Sharma, R., Joshi, R., & Shah, C. (2009). *Approaches to the lands for the urban poor.* Centre for Urban Equity, Working Paper 2.

Majale, M. (2008). Employment creation through participatory urban planning and slum upgrading: The case of Kitale, Kenya. *Habitat International, 32,* 270–282.

Marcuse, P. (1992). Why conventional self-help projects won't work. In K. Mathey (Ed.), *Beyond self-help housing* (pp. 15–22). London and New York: Profil Verlag.

Mascarenhas, A. (2010, July 18). *Survey to find if slum dwellers willing to pay for affordable homes.* Retrieved October 11, 2013, from The Indian Express (Online Edition) Pune: www.indianexpress.com/news/survey-to-find-if-slum-dwellers-willing-to-pay-for-affordable-homes/648087/

MoHUPA. (2009). *Guidelines for affordable housing in partnership* (JNNURM Mission Directorate). New Delhi: Ministry of Housing & Urban Poverty Alleviation, Government of India.

REFERENCES

MoHUPA. (2013). *New guidelines for affordable housing in partnership.* (JNNURM Mission Directorate). New Delhi: Ministry of Housing & Urban Poverty Alleviation, Government of India.

MoHUPA, GoI. (1988). *National Housing and Habitat Policy 1998: An overview.* Retrieved June 24, 2014, from http://mhupa.gov.in/: http://mhupa.gov.in/policies/duepa/nhhp.htm

MoHUPA, GoI. (2007). *National Urban Housing and Habitat Policy (NUHHP), 2007.* New Delhi: Ministry of Housing & Urban Poverty Alleviation, GoI.

MoHUPA, GoI. (2012a). *Report of the Task Force on Promoting Affordable Housing, 2012.* New Delhi: Ministry of Housing & Urban Poverty Alleviation, Government of India.

MoHUPA, GoI. (2012b, November 14). *Revision of income ceilings for EWS and LIG: MoHUPA order.* Retrieved July 15, 2014, from Ministry of Housing and Urban Poverty Alleviation – Housing Division: http://mhupa.gov.in/W_new/EWS_OFFICE_MEMORUNDUM_14_11_2012.pdf

MoHUPA, GoI. (2012c, October). [Document Ref: No.N-11025/40/2010-UCD]. *Expression of Interest (EoI) to undertake the task of revision of the Urban Development Plan Formulation and Implementation (UDPFI) guidelines, 1996.* New Delhi.

MoHUPA, NBO, GoI. (2012). *Report of the Technical Group on Urban Housing Shortage (TG-12) (2012–17).* New Delhi: Ministry of Housing and Urban Poverty Alleviation, National Buildings Organisation, Government of India.

McKinsey Global Institute. (2010). *India's urban awakening: Building inclusive cities, sustaining economic growth.* McKinsey & Company. Retrieved from https://www.mckinsey.com/featured-insights/urbanization/urban-awakening-in-india

Mukherji, A., & Bharucha, N. K. (2011, August 13). *Realty bites: House in Mumbai slums for Rs 40 lakh.* Retrieved June 3, 2014, from The Times of India, Mumbai: http://timesofindia.indiatimes.com/city/mumbai/Realty-bites-House-in-Mumbai-slums-for-Rs-40-lakh/articleshow/9585639.cms

Mukhija, V. (2001). Enabling slum redevelopment in Mumbai: Policy paradox in practice. *Housing Studies, 16*(6), 791–806.

Mukhopadhyay, P. (2008, May 18). *Falling through the cracks: India's failing infrastructure policy.* Retrieved June 12, 2014, from Center for the Advanced Study of India (CASI): http://casi.sas.upenn.edu/iit/mukhopadhyay

NAHC. (2015). *Buying into a housing cooperative.* Retrieved June 10, 2015, from National Association of Housing Cooperatives (NAHC): http://coophousing.org/resources/owning-a-cooperative/buying-into-a-housing-cooperative/

National Housing Bank. (2006). *Report on trend & progress of housing in India, 2006.* India: National Housing Bank.

Navarro, M. (2015, April 20). *88,000 applicants and counting for 55 units in 'poor door' building.* Retrieved May 13, 2015, from The New York Times: www.nytimes.com/2015/04/21/nyregion/poor-door-building-draws-88000-applicants-for-55-rental-units.html?smid=tw-nytimes&_r=1

NCDF. (n.d.). *Housing cooperatives: An accessible and lasting tool for home ownership* (N. C. Fund, Ed.). Retrieved June 10, 2015, from www.uwcc.wisc.edu/pdf/HousingCoopsAccessibleLastingHomeOwnership.pdf

NDTV. (2014, July 10). *Arun Jaitley wants home EMIs to be cheaper than rent.* Retrieved July 15, 2014, from http://profit.ndtv.com/: http://profit.ndtv.com/budget/arun-jaitley-wants-home-emis-to-be-cheaper-than-rent-586663

Needham, B., & de Kam, G. (2000). *Land for social housing.* Nijmegen: CECODHAS.

Needham, B., & de Kam, G. (2004, September). Understanding how land is exchanged: Co-ordination mechanisms and transaction costs. *Urban Studies, 41*(10), 2061–2076.

NHB. (1999). *The National Housing & Habitat Policy-1998: An overview.* Retrieved June 24, 2014, from Report on Trend and Progress of Housing in India – June, 1999: www.nhb.org.in/Publications/trends_nhhp.php

NHB. (2006). *Report on trend & progress of housing in India, 2006.* New Delhi: National Housing Bank. Retrieved from https://www.nhb.org.in/Publications/Trends_Progress_Report2006.pdf

NHB. (2012a). *Report on trend and progress of housing in India, 2012.* New Delhi: National Housing Bank.

NHB. (2012b, April 25). *Home loan Interest rates from leading Primary Lending Institutions in India.* Retrieved September 1, 2014, from National Housing Bank [housingindia.info]: www.housingindia.info/NHBHomeLoanRates.aspx

NJ AES. (n.d.). *What is a Transfer of Development Rights (TDR) program?* Retrieved August 2014, 26, from rutgers.edu – New Jersey Agricultural Experiment Program: http://njaes.rutgers.edu/highlands/tdr.asp

North, D. C. (1990a). Institutions and a transaction-cost theory of exchange. In J. E. Alt & K. A. Shepsle (Eds.), *Perspectives on positive political economy* (pp. 182–194, Chapter 7). Cambridge: Cambridge University Press.

North, D. C. (1990b). *Institutions, institutional change and economic performance.* Cambridge: Cambridge University Press.

North, D. C. (1993a). *New institutional economics and development.* Working Paper, St. Louis: Washington University.

North, D. C. (1993b, December 9). *Economic performance through time – Nobel Prize Lecture –1993.* Retrieved October 13, 2014, from www.nobelprize.org/: www.nobelprize.org/nobel_prizes/economic-sciences/laureates/1993/north-lecture.html

Panchu, S., & Rastogi, A. (2013). The battle between corruption and governance in India: Strategies for tipping the scale. In H. Cisse, N. M. Menon, M.-C. Segger, & V. Nmehielle (Eds.), *The World Bank Legal Review, Volume 5: Fostering development through opportunity, inclusion, and equity* (pp. 381–398). Washington, DC: The World Bank Group.

Paul, S., & Shah, M. (1997). Corruption in public service delivery. In S. Guhan & P. Samuel (Eds.), *Corruption in India: Agenda for action* (pp. 144–163). New Delhi: Public Affairs Centre.

Payne, G. K. (1977). *Urban housing in the third world.* London and Boston, MA: Leonard Hill, Routledge & Kegan Paul.

Payne, G. K. (2001a). Urban land tenure policy options: Titles or rights?. *Habitat International, 25*(3), 415–429.

Payne, G. K. (2001b). Lowering the ladder: Regulatory frameworks for sustainable development. *Development in Practice, 11*(2–3).

The Planning Commission. (2011). *The challenges of urbanization in India: Approach to the 12.* New Delhi: The Planning Commission, GoI.

Planning Commission, GoI. (1992). *8th Five Year Plan*. New Delhi: Government of India.

Policy Link. (2003). *Expanding housing opportunity in Washington, DC: The case for inclusionary zoning*. New York: A PolicyLink Report.

Powell, B., & Stringham, E. (2005). The economics of inclusionary zoning reclaimed: How effective are price controls? *Florida State University Law Review, 33*, 471–499.

Prasad, K. (2014, June 4). *Chandrababu Naidu to waive off farm loans totalling Rs 54,000 crore*. Retrieved June 10, 2014, from The Times of India: http://timesofindia.indiatimes.com/india/Chandrababu-Naidu-to-waive-off-farm-loans-totalling-Rs-54000-crore/articleshow/36026189.cms

Press Trust India. (2012, November 22). *SP waives off loans of 7.2 lakh farmers as Mulayam's birthday gift*. Retrieved June 10, 2014, from India Today: http://indiatoday.intoday.in/story/sp-waives-off-loans-of-7.2-lakh-farmers-maybe-its-mulayams-birthday-effect/1/230365.html

PRIA. (2012, October 3). *"Poor living" for the urban poor: Tracing JNNURM housing projects*. Terra Urban. Raipur: Participatory Research in Asia (PRIA).

Rajan, R. (2013). *Statement by Dr. Raghuram Rajan on taking office on September 4, 2013*. Retrieved August 11, 2014, from Reserve Bank of India: http://rbi.org.in/scripts/BS_PressReleaseDisplay.aspx?prid=29479

Rolnik, R. (2012, November 14). *Financialisation of housing and the right to adequate housing*. Retrieved June 17, 2014, from Think Africa Press: http://thinkafricapress.com/international-law-africa/housing

Rossi, A. (2011, December 13). *Slum dwellers priced out as shacks hit £50k*. Retrieved June 3, 2014, from Sky News: http://news.sky.com/story/908753/slum-dwellers-priced-out-as-shacks-hit-50k

Roth, A. E. (2007, October). The art of designing markets. *Harvard Business Review, 85*(10), 118.

Sandhu, K., & Korzeniewski, S. (2004). The impact of neoliberal ideology on housing policy and practice. *ITPI Journal, 1*(4), 1–7.

Sanyal, B., & Mukhija, V. (2001). Institutional pluralism and housing delivery: A case of unforeseen conflicts in Mumbai, India. *World Development, 29*(12), 2043–2057.

Satyanarayana, V. (2001, March). *Milestones in development of municipal bond market in India*. Retrieved June 12, 2014, from Ministry of Urban Development: www.urbanindia.nic.in/legislations/li_by_min/Model_Municipal_Law/chap30.pdf

Sengupta, U., & Tipple, A. G. (2007, September). The performance of public-sector housing in Kolkata, India, in the post-reform milieu. *Urban Studies, 44*(10), 2009–2027. https://doi.org/10.1080/00420980701471927

Shelter UK. (2015a). *How councils decide priority for social housing*. Retrieved May 13, 2015, from Shelter – The housing and homelessness charity: http://england.shelter.org.uk/get_advice/social_housing/applying_for_social_housing/who_gets_priority

Shelter UK. (2015b). *What is local housing allowance (LHA)?* Retrieved May 13, 2015, from Shelter – The Housing and Homeless Charity: http://england.shelter.org.uk/get_advice/housing_benefit_and_local_housing_allowance/what_is_housing_benefit/local_housing_allowance

Singh, N. (1998, July 20). *CM as Santa: Madhya Pradesh CM Digvijay Singh hits campaign trail armed with sops, schemes.* Retrieved July 15, 2013, from India Today: http://indiatoday.intoday.in/story/madhya-pradesh-cm-digvijay-singh-hits-campaign-trail-armed-with-sops-schemes/1/264573.html

Singh, S. (2011a, February 25). *We used the Right to Information Act to expose several housing frauds* (V. Babout, Interviewer). New Delhi: Times of India.

Singh, S. (2011b, January). *Rethinking low incoming housing in India.* Retrieved from www.designwala.org: www.designwala.org/2011/01/rethinking-low-incoming-housing-in-india/

Sivam, A., & Karuppannan, S. (2002). Role of state and market in housing delivery for low income groups in India. *Journal of Housing and the Built Environment,* 69–88.

Sliogeris, E., Crabtree, L., Phibbs, P., Johnston, K., & O'Neill, P. (2008). *Housing affordability literature review and affordable housing program audit.* Retrieved from https://researchdirect.westernsydney.edu.au/islandora/object/uws:11827/datastream/PDF/view

Smets, P. (2002). Indian housing finance alliances and the urban poor. *Global Built Environment Review,* 2(2), 58–66.

Stokes, S. C., Dunning, T., Nazareno, M., & Brusco, V. (2013). *Brokers, voters, and clientelism: The puzzle of distributive politics.* Cambridge Studies in Comparative Politics. Cambridge: Cambridge University Press.

Taylor-Robinson, M. M. (2010). *Do the poor count? Democratic institutions and accountability in a context of poverty.* University Park, PA: The Pennsylvania State University Press.

Technical Committee Chaired by Dr. Pronab Sen. (2010). *Report of the Committee on Slum Statistics.* New Delhi: National Building Organization and Ministry of Housing and Urban Poverty Alleviation, Government of India.

Thakur, P. (2009, June 22). *India pays penalty for not utilising loans from lending agencies.* Retrieved June 12, 2014, from The Times of India: http://timesofindia.india-times.com/India/India-pays-penalty-for-not-utilising-loans-from-lending-agencies/articleshow/4684437.cms

Thangavel, C. (1998). Income and rent affordability of economically weaker sections in Madras. In *Affordable housing and infrastructure in India* (pp. 84–91). New Delhi: Reliance Publishing House.

Tipple, D. A., & Majale, D. M. (2006). *Enabling shelter strategies: Review of experience from two decades of implementation.* Nairobi: UN-HABITAT.

Topalova, P. (2005). *Trade liberalization, poverty, and inequality: Evidence from Indian districts.* Cambridge, MA: National Bureau of Economic Research.

Turner, J. C. (1968). Housing priorities, settlement patterns, and urban development in modernizing countries. *Journal of the American Institute of Planners,* 34(6), 354–363.

Twelfth Finance Commission. (2004). *Report of the Twelfth Finance Commission (2005–2010).* New Delhi: Government of India.

UN-ECE. (2005). *Housing finance systems for countries in transition: Principles and examples.* Economic Commission for Europe. New York and Geneva: United Nations.

UN-ESCAP. (1998). *Urban land policies for the uninitiated.* Retrieved January 19, 2013, from United Nations Economic and Social Commission for Asia and the Pacific: www.unescap.org/huset/land_policies/

United Nations Human Settlements Programme (UN-HABITAT). (2003). *The challenge of slums: Global report on human settlements 2003*. Nairobi, Kenya: United Nations Human Settlements Programme (UN-HABITAT).

United Nations Human Settlements Programme (UN-HABITAT). (2011). *Affordable land and Housing in Asia*. Nairobi, Kenya: United Nations Human Settlements Programme (UN-HABITAT).

van der Linden, J. J. (1986). *The sites and services approach reviewed: Solution or stopgap to the Third World housing shortage?* Aldershot: Gower Publishing Company.

Vasumathi, P. (2018). A study of home buyer's awareness on Real Estate Regulation and Development Act (RERA) in Chennai city, Tamilnadu, India. *Oman Chapter of Arabian Journal of Business and Management Review*, 34(6109), 1–6.

Verma, G. D. (2002). *Slumming India: A chronicle of slums and their saviours*. Retrieved from Egully.com

Wagner, R. H. (1988). Economic interdependence, bargaining power, and political influence. *International Organization*, 42(3), 461–483.

WIEGO. (n.d.). *Street vendors in India*. Retrieved February 18, 2014, from Women in Informal Employment: Globalizing and Organizing (WIEGO): http://wiego.org/informal_economy_law/street-vendors-india

Williamson, O. E. (1993). Transaction cost economics and organization theory. *Industrial and Corporate Change*, 2(2), 107–156.

Willis, K. G., & Tipple, A. G. (1991). Introduction to housing analysis and an overview. In K. G. Willis & A. G. Tipple (Eds.), *Housing the poor in the developing world: Methods of analysis, case studies and policy* (pp. 1–16). London and New York: Routledge.

Working group on Construction Sector for Planning Commission (2012–17). (2011). *Report of the Working Group on Construction for the 11th Five Year Plan (2012–2017)*. New Delhi: Government of India.

The World Bank. (1988). *The emerging role of housing finance*. Washington, DC: The Urban Development Division, The World Bank.

The World Bank. (1991). *Urban policy and economic development: An agenda for the 1990s*. Washington, DC: The World Bank.

The World Bank. (1993). *Housing enabling markets to work: A World Bank policy paper*. Washington, DC: The World Bank.

The World Bank. (1997). *World development report 1997: The state in a changing world*. Washington, DC: Published by Oxford University Press for The International Bank for Reconstruction and Development/The World Bank.

The World Bank. (2000). *World Bank urban and local government strategy*. Urban Development, Infrastructure Group. Washington, DC: The International Bank for Reconstruction and Development/The World Bank.

World Bank. (2009). *Doing bussiness in India*. Washington, DC: World Bank and the International Finance Corporation.

World Bank. Office of Environmental Affairs. (1974). *Environmental, health and human ecologic considerations in economic development projects*. Washington, DC: World Bank.

Zérah, M.-H. (2009, September). Participatory governance in urban management and the shifting geometry of power in Mumbai. *Development and Change*, 40(5), 853–877.

INDEX

Note: Page numbers in *italic* indicate a *figure* and page numbers in **bold** indicate a **table** on the corresponding page; Page numbers followed by 'n' refer to notes.